Performance Training for Golf

Sean Cochran

SMC Publishing

Performance Training for Golf

Published by
SMC Publishing
12368 Carmel Country Rd. Suite D103
San Diego, CA 92130

Copyright © 2015 SMC Publishing, San Diego, California

Published by SMC Publishing, San Diego, California

No part of this publication may be reproduced, stored in a retrieval system, or transmitted in any form or by any means, electronic, mechanical, photocopying, recording, scanning, or otherwise, except as permitted under Sections 107 or 108 of the 1976 United States Copyright Act, without either the prior written permission of the Publisher, or authorization through payment of the appropriate per-copy fee to SMC Publishing 858-350-9165. Requests to the Publisher for permission should be addressed to Legal Department, SMC Publishing, 510 Stratford Ct. Suite 305A, Del Mar, CA 92014, or e-mail at support@seancochran.com

LIMITS OF LIABILITY/DISCLAIMER OF WARRANTY: WHILE THE PUBLISHER AND AUTHOR HAVE USED THEIR BEST EFFORTS IN PREPARING THIS BOOK, THEY MAKE NO REPRESENTATION OR WARRANTIES OF ACCURACY OR COMPLETENESS OF THE CONTENTS OF THIS BOOK. THE ADVICE AND STRATEGIES CONTAINED HEREIN MAY NOT BE SUITABLE FOR YOUR SITUATION. YOU SHOULD CONSULT WITH A PROFESSIONAL WHERE APPROPRIATE. SOME OF THE EXERCISES AND DIETARY SUGGESTIONS CONTAINED HEREIN MAY NOT BE APPROPRIATE FOR ALL INDIVIDUALS, AND CONSULTATION WITH A PHYSCIAN IS SUGGESTED BEFORE COMMENCING ANY EXERCISE OR DIETARY PROGRAM. NEITHER THE PUBLISHER NOR AUTHOR SHALL BE LIABLE FOR ANY LOSS OF PROFIT OR ANY COMMERCIAL DAMAGES INCLUDING BUT NOT LIMITED TO SPECIAL, INCIDENTAL, CONSEQUENTIAL, OR OTHER DAMAGES.

For general information on our other products and services or to obtain technical support, please contact us at 858-350-9165 or e-mail support@seancochran.com

Manufactured in the United States of America.

This book is dedicated to my parents, friends, mentors, athletes, and coaches who have assisted me throughout this great career, thank you.

Also by Sean Cochran

Complete Conditioning for Pitchers

Fit to Hit

Strength Ball Training for Sports Performance

Success in Professional Athletics

Complete Conditioning for Martial Arts

Stronger Arms and Upper Body (with Dr. Tom House)

Contents

Introduction		5
Chapter 1	*Biomechanics of the Golf Swing*	6
Chapter 2	*Exercise Science*	16
Chapter 3	*Training Principles*	21
Chapter 4	*Assessment*	30
Chapter 5	*Mobility & Flexibility Exercises*	50
Chapter 6	*Corrective & Warm Up Exercises*	73
Chapter 7	*Balance Exercises*	92
Chapter 8	*Power Training*	108
Chapter 9	*Core Exercises*	127
Chapter 10	*Functional Strength Exercises*	148
Chapter 11	*Anaerobic Training, Aerobics, Nutrition, & Recovery*	177
Chapter 12	*Strength & Conditioning Programs*	182
About the Author		198

Introduction

As I have stated in assorted books, articles, and publications: The golf swing is one of the most intricate and difficult athletic movements in sports today. It requires the golfer to perform a specific set of movements in the correct sequence and timing. Any error in timing, sequence, or positioning of these movements will invariably cause an error in the execution of the golf swing. In order to execute the movements of the golf swing correctly, certain levels of mobility, flexibility, balance, stability, strength, endurance, and power are required.

What I have found in over my 15 years in professional athletics, training of the professional and recreational athlete the body (i.e. kinetic chain) does not always have the physical capabilities developed within it to execute a biomechanically efficient golf swing. The result of these physical deficiencies can cause a vast number of compensations to occur during the execution of the golf swing. Results of such compensations are quantified in a lack of club head speed, face angle errors, misdirection of shots, poor ball striking, injuries, and in general less than optimal performance on the course.

The typical plan of attack to correct swing faults, improve ball striking, increase club head speed, and alleviate injuries often times centers upon increased swing instruction and practice sessions. This is a mistake, because the root of many problems does not ie within the golf swing, but within the body itself. More often than not, the golfer does not have the physical structure developed within his/her body to execute the golf swing, and as stated above, this causes a lengthy list of compensations to occur during the execution of the golf swing.

To address the physical requirements of the golf swing, the golfer athlete can take steps to develop the required levels of flexibility, strength, and power required to execute a biomechanically sound golf swing. These steps are in the form of a strength and conditioning program centered on the physical requirement of the golf swing. Such a program will develop the physical components of the body (kinetic chain) specifically to the needs and requirements of the golf swing, allowing for the creation of the physical foundation needed for a biomechanically efficient golf swing. The end result of such training will be increases in club head speeds, improved ball striking capabilities, less potential for injury, improved stamina, and ultimately lower scores.

The mission of *Performance Training for Golf* is to provide you with the information and tools to develop your body in order to advance your golf game. The process by which we will accomplish this is through improving the flexibility, mobility, balance capacities, strength, and power outputs of your body. This, in combination with proper instruction, and constructive practice sessions will elevate your golf game.

Chapter One

Biomechanics of the Golf Swing

Biomechanics is the sport science field that applies the laws of mechanics and physics to human performance, in order to gain a greater understanding of performance in athletic events through modeling, simulation and measurement. Great strides have been made in the field of biomechanical analysis of golf swing. These advancements are providing the golfing community with great insight into the kinematics, neuromuscular firing patterns, and physical requirements of the golf swing.

Leaders in the data capture on the biomechanics of the golf swing over the past 15 years have been the Titleist Performance Institute headed by Dr. Greg Rose, Advanced Motion Measurements directed by Dr. Phil Cheetham, and the American Sports Medicine Institute founded by Dr. James Andrews. Through research by these companies we have learned a vast amount of information about the correlation between the biomechanics of the golf swing and the human body. We now know how golfers generate speed (i.e. power), transfer energy through the body to the club, and ultimately what a biomechanically efficient golf swing looks like.

Kinematic Sequence

The goal of the golf swing is to strike the golf ball achieving maximum distance with a high level of accuracy, and minimal stress on the body. Through biomechanical studies of the golf swing, a model has been developed to determine the efficiency at which this occurs within the human body. This model is referred to as the kinematic sequence of the golf swing. (Rose Greg, Titleist Performance Institute Manual, 10) The kinematic sequence allows a viewer to look at how efficiently and effectively a golfer generates speed, transfers speed through the body, and where in the golf swing a golfer may lack the physical or biomechanical requirements to execute the swing with the greatest amount of efficiency possible.

Studies on the biomechanics of the golf swing and development of the kinematic sequence has provided the following key points about the golf swing. According to Dr. Greg Rose of TPI, the kinematic sequence indicates the following points:

1) All great ball strikers have an identical sequence of generating speed and transferring energy through the kinetic chain (i.e. body) to the club. This sequence is as follows: lower body first, torso second, lead arm third, and club last. This sequence occurs within the downswing. Any deviation within this sequencing will cause a loss of speed and a decrease in the transfer of energy. For example, the lower body will begin the downswing, followed by the torso, lead arm, and completed when the clubface impacts the golf ball. If the torso were to precede the lower body in this sequence, the generation of speed and the transfer of energy would be compromised.

2) Each segment of the body (lower body, torso, lead arm) builds upon the previous segment thus increasing speed as it moves up the kinetic chain to the club. For example, speed generated from the lower body is transferred to the torso, where the speed is increased from the recruitment of the torso, and then again transferred to the lead arm where speed is again increased.

3) Each segment of the kinetic chain (i.e. lower body, torso, lead arm) slows down after the energy is transferred to the next segment as it is accelerating further. For example, once the lower body transfers the speed it has developed to the torso, the lower body must slow down for an efficient transfer of this energy to occur as well as for the kinematic sequence to remain intact.

Understanding the kinematic sequence is imperative to the development of a biomechanically sound golf swing. The information provided by the kinematic sequence allows us to determine where a golfer generates speed within the golf swing, what if any segments of the kinetic chain are limiting the transfer of energy in the golf swing, possible areas of the body being overused or stressed in the swing, and what areas of the body or swing require attention for improvement within the golfer's swing.

Kinematic Sequence

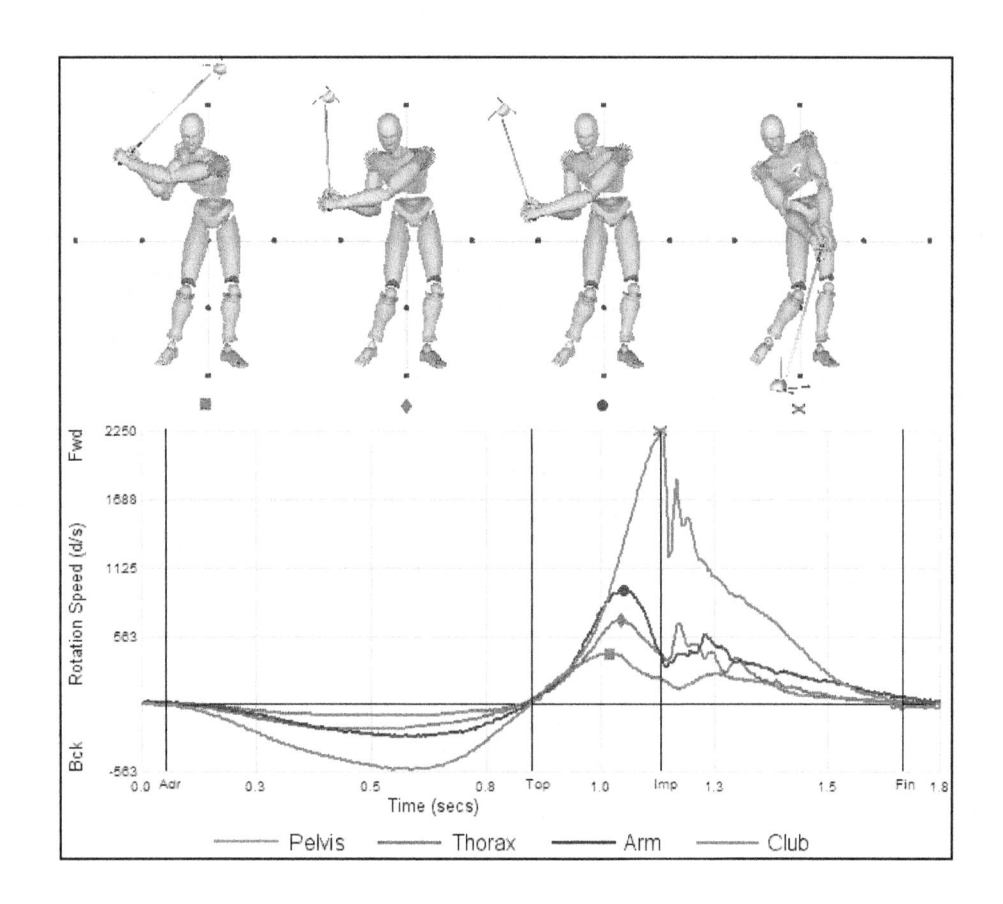

Phases of the Golf Swing

Through biomechanical studies by the American Sports Medicine Institute (ASMI) located in Birmingham, Alabama a sequential model of the golf swing has been developed. Through the utilization of this model in conjunction with the kinematic sequence we can review the golf swing and determine the necessary physical requirements of the body for the execution of a biomechanically efficient golf swing in which the kinematic sequence remains intact. ASMI has broken down the golf swing into the following "series of biomechanical movements":

1) Set-up

2) Backswing

3) Transition

4) Downswing

5) Impact

6) Follow-through

In order to better understand the connection between the kinematic sequence, golf swing, the body, and the interaction of these three entities, we will look at each phase of the golf swing from a biomechanical perspective.

Set-up

The set-up position often referred to as the "address" position, is the position in which the golfer places the body to begin the golf swing. According to Glenn Fleisig, M.D., the set-up position is a functional body position, that includes the proper grip. A balanced, "athletic" address position, which is consistent swing to swing, will provide the golfer with the correct starting position for the swing. According to Leadbetter and Huggan, a slight variation in weight distribution should be present when using different length clubs. The hips should be aligned in the direction of the target, while the right shoulder (right handed golfer) should be dropped slightly. The knees and hips should be comfortably flexed, resulting in the right shoulder being approximately directly above the right foot. Inconsistency in either how the body is set up or with the grip leads to inconsistency from shot to shot.

The body, in terms of muscle activity, is fairly low at address. The muscles of the body are supporting the body in a specific anatomical position and preparing to swing the club. Even though muscle activity is low at address, certain levels of joint mobility, muscular flexibility, and stability are required of the kinetic chain in order to position itself in the correct set-up position.

The set up for golfer's of any level can often be the position in which many swing faults can be traced back too. Improper placement of the body prior to execution of the golf swing will directly lead to re-routing of the club, poor sequencing, and the development of numerous compensations in the golf swing. Typically, the cause for an improper address position will be from either poor mobility (i.e. flexibility) in specific joints or a lack of stability (i.e. strength) in certain body segments.

GolfToday.com

Backswing

The backswing is when the body begins to move the club. The backswing is the portion of the swing placing the body in the correct position to begin the downswing. During the entire backswing the body begins the recruitment of energy that will be transitioned at the top of the backswing towards the ball. Key points from a biomechanical analysis of the backswing are: as the club moves backwards shear force is applied to the anterior portion of the right foot while at the same time a posterior shear force is applied to the left foot. (Fleisig, Biomechanics of Golf) This is the beginning of torque development in the body (i.e. kinetic chain) that will be transitioned into the clubhead at impact. Rotation of the knees, hips, spine, and shoulders continues during the backswing. The order of this rotation is the knees, hips, and torso occurring around an approximate vertical axis through the center of the body. This creates additional torque to be translated into the clubhead in later stages of the swing. The important point to remember in the backswing is that the entire rotation of these body parts occurs around an imaginary axis of the body. The body during this portion of the swing is creating/storing energy to be released during the downswing phase of the golf swing.

An important point to remember in the backswing is that the entire rotation of these body parts occurs around an imaginary axis of the body. The body during this portion of the swing is creating/storing energy to be released towards the end of the swing.

The biomechanical analysis of the backswing indicates this is the stage of the swing at which speed development begins. The process by which this occurs is through the creation of torque and the development of torque by the body requires rotation. Rotation in the lower body, torso, and shoulders is contingent upon a number of physical parameters such as joint range of motion, muscular extensibility, stretch reflex, and segmental strength in the lower body, hips, core, and upper back. If any of these physical entities are lacking, the ability to execute the backswing and develop torque will be diminished.

BigStockPhoto.com

Transition

The completion of the backswing is termed the "transition" stage of the swing. The transition point of the swing is where the body completes its backward movement and begins the forward movement. The best reference point to when the transition stage of the swing begins is when weight shift onto the inside of the right foot is completed (right-handed golfers) and movement back towards the left foot begins. Research indicates the transition of the swing is where additional elastic energy is stored within the body. This is a result of the lower body moving forward as the upper body continues to "coil" backward (i.e. "X-factor). Studies show at the completion of the transition (top of the backswing) the hips are closed approximately 45 degrees and the shoulders are closed to about 100 degrees. (Fleisig, Biomechanics of Golf)

The transition phase of the golf swing as with every other phase of the golf swing requires specified levels of joint mobility and segmental stability. Limitations in thoracic spine or hip mobility will typically result in compensations or inefficient movement patterns to occur at this stage of the golf swing. In addition, an inability to stabilize the lumbo/pelvic/hip complex will negate the ability to maintain the correct postural position required in the initiation of the downswing phase.

Downswing

After completion of the transition, the downswing begins. Weight shift continues during the downswing. The generation of torque is created in the lower body and then is transitioned up through the body into the club. The majority of torque in this phase of the swing is generated by the glutes, hamstrings, quadrcieps, and lumbo-pelvic-hip complex musculature of the body. (Fleisig, Biomechanics of Golf) The torque created in the lower body creates acceleration in the upper body as energy is transferred onto the clubhead. Studies indicate there is moderate muscular activity in the pectoralis major (chest), latissimus dorsi (upper back), and rotator cuff muscles during the downswing. (Geisler, Kinesiology of the Full Golf Swing) The downswing is complete at the point in which impact occurs with the golf ball.

Studies by McCarrol and Gioe's indicate there are 50% more injuries in the downswing as backswing. Explanation for this increase in injury during this phase of the swing is believed to be a result of the golf club covering the same range of motion as in the backswing but in a significantly less amount of time. (Fleisig, The Biomechanics of Golf)

A model commonly used to demonstrate the biomechanics of the downswing is referred to as a double pendulum. This pendulum consists of an upper and lower pendulum. The upper pendulum represents a link between the two wrists on the club and either the left shoulder or a point between the two shoulders. (Fleisig, Analysis of a Mechanical Model of the Golf Swing) The lower pendulum represents the represents the club from the wrists to clubhead. (Milburn, PD, Summation of segmental velocities of the golf swing)

Downswing - Upper Pendulum Acceleration

After completion of the transition stage and commencement of the downswing, the golfer will continue the weight shift onto the left foot through movement of the pelvis toward the intended target line. During this movement of the kinetic chain force is applied onto the anterior portion of the right foot and posterior side of the left foot, which in turn generates a counterclockwise torque (right handed golfer). (Carlsoo, S, A kinetic analysis of the golf swing) The torque generated by the lower body is transferred to the torso with an additional amount of energy supplied by the musculature of the lumbo/pelvic/hip complex. (McCarrol, JR, Sports Injuries: Mechanisms, Prevention, and Treatment) This additional torque provided by the lumbo/pelvic/hip complex creates a counterclockwise acceleration of the upper pendulum. In addition, muscular of the upper pendulum concentrically active during the downswing were eccentrically loaded during the backswing.

Final notes of the upper pendulum is muscular of the right and left shoulder are contributing to speed generation. In addition, a negative torque by the wrists remaining radially deviated during the early stages prevents the lower pendulum from opening and maximum dorsiflexion of the right wrist (right handed golfer) occurs when the club is approximately horizontal to the ground. (Milburn, Summation of segmental velocities in the golf swing)

Downswing - Lower Pendulum Acceleration

The lower pendulum of the downswing is initiated once the club has reached a parallel position to the ground. At this position ulnar deviation of the wrists occur sequentially allowing the left forearm to supinate and right forearm to pronate, commonly referred to as a "knuckles down" move. (Hay, JG, The Biomechanics of Sports Technique) At this stage the release of the wrists begins the acceleration of the lower pendulum and sequential deceleration of the upper pendulum. (Hay, JG, The Biomechanics of Sports Technique)

The mechanics of the lower pendulum is directed by the pectoralis major, subscapularis, latisimus dorsi, and the arms. (Milburn, PD, Summation of segemental velocities in the golf swing) Motion analysis of the golf swing indicates maintaining clubshaft-to-left arm angle into the latter stages of the downswing allows a great summation of forces by the upper pendulum due to low moment of interia. (Leadbetter D, and Huggan, J, The

Golf Swing) The less skilled golfer will not maintain this clubshaft-arm angle typically referred to as casting and as a result loose a substantial amount of speed.

Keeping the kinematic sequence in place during the downswing allows for the generation and transfer of speed into the golf ball. In order for this to occur, high levels of neuromuscular efficiency, strength, mobility, and power are required in the lower body, core, and upper body. In addition, the transfer of energy via the kinetic chain to the club requires efficiency within the process of accelerating and decelerating kinetic chain segments. This component requires a foundation of inter-muscular and intra-muscular coordination to exist within the kinetic chain. This allows for power to be generated by each of these segments, transferred efficiently to the next segment of the kinetic chain and also allows for each of these segments to decelerate once energy has been transferred to next.

BigStockPhoto.com

Impact

Impact is the point at which the potential energy/speed generated by the body during the backswing, transition, and downswing is transferred into the golf ball. Impact with the ball occurs for approximately half a millisecond. (Fleisig, Biomechanics of Golf) The purpose of impact is to hit the ball in the correct direction with the chosen amount of force.

At impact, weight transfer is complete and shear forces from both feet are towards the intended target. The clubhead and ball at impact are in contact for approximately half a millisecond (0.0005 seconds). Any error in timing, positioning of the kinetic chain, sequencing of the swing, or positioning of the clubface will directly affect the impact position, ball flight, speed, and direction.

Biomechanically at the impact position the counterclockwise rotation of the feet is complete. Research indicates at impact the left foot (right-handed golfer) is supporting 80% to 95% of the golfer's weight. (Fleisig, Biomechanics of Golf) In addition to the percentage of weight shift, research has found the lower handicap golfer had their weight supported toward the heel of the left foot, whereas the higher handicapper supported the weight in the middle of the foot. (Richards, J, Weight transfer patterns during the golf swing) The hypothesis behind this differentiation at impact between the lower and higher handicapper was the skilled golfer obtains more counterclockwise rotation during the swing.

Maximum clubhead speed is intended to occur at the impact position. Higher handicap players due to biomechanical inefficiencies and or physical dysfunctions loose speed prior to impact resulting in a loss of distance and potential ball flight direction.

Execution of the impact postion requires the release of the hands with correct timing for the transfer of speed to the club head. In order to perform the wrist release, weight shift correctly, sequence the transfer of energy through the body, and release speed into the golf ball, all phases of the golf swing leading up to this point must be executed correctly. Errors in the kinematic sequence or phases of the golf swing caused by physical limitations, poor mechanics, or improper equipment will affect impact. Physical dysfunctions in terms of mobility, flexibility, stability, strength and/or power development will "show up" at impact relative to ball flight, distance, and direction.

BigStockPhoto.com

Follow-Through

After contact, the impact stage of the swing is complete and the follow through stage begins. The follow through is essentially the deceleration of the body after contact with the ball has been made. This is completed with the body rotating to a completion point where the clubhead is behind the golfer. The follow through is where the kinematic sequence of the swing ends, energy not transferred into the golf ball is dissipated, and the body slows itself back down. It is the deceleration phase of the golf swing.

Biomechanically after impact with the golf ball the left forearm (right handed golfer) continues to supinate, the right forearm continues to pronate, pelvis and thoracic spine rotations concludes. Deceleration of the kinetic chain requires activation of the subscapularis, latissimus dorsi, and pectoralis major. In addition, both legs rotate as the right knee flexes and left ankle suppinates. (McCarroll, JR and Gioe, TJ, Professional golfers and the price they pay) The right heel will lifted off the ground during the follow through positioning the majority of the vertical load on the left foot (right handed golfer). (McCarroll, JR, Sports Injuries: Mechanisms, Prevention, and Treatment)

Deceleration of the kinetic chain during the follow phase of the golf swing requires a high level of eccentric and stabilization strength of the muscular system. This allows for dissipation of energy not translated into the club head and a slowing down of the body. Poor conditioning of the neuromuscular system or limited joint ranges of motion may limit the ability of the golfer to execute this phase of the golf swing efficiently.

BigStockPhoto.com

Summary

Information on the kinematic sequence and biomechanics of the golf swing provides an insurmountable amount of information about the golf swing. These segments of information provide any golfer, swing coach, or conditioning coach with a great deal of insight on how speed is developed in the swing, how energy is transferred to the clubhead, what is physically required of the body to perform the golf swing efficiently, and where the swing may be "short circuiting".
At this point we have a understanding of the connection between the body and execution of the golf swing. We know limitations in mobility, flexibility, neuromuscular efficiency, stability, and/or power will cause limitations in the execution of a biomechanically efficient golf swing, increase the potential for injury, as well as negatively affect the kinematic sequence. As you can see each and every phase requires specific levels of mobility, neuromuscular efficiency, stability, and power to execute correctly.

As stated previously, we can correct physical limitations in the areas of flexibility, strength, endurance, and power through the implementation of a strength and conditioning program for golf. Over time, improvements can be made physically with such a program assisting you in executing a biomechanically efficient golf swing.

As you can see from the above table the human body "feet to fingertips" operates in an alternating pattern of a mobile joint followed by a stable joint throughout the entire kinetic chain (i.e. body). It is obvious joints such as the elbow and knee are not rod like pieces of iron that do not flex or extend, but rather these joints are stable in terms of limited degrees of motion. For example, the knee joint does not rotate in 360 degrees of motion as does the hip or shoulder, rather it operates essentially in one plane of motion flexing and extending. As a result this joint is considered a stable joint where as the hip, shoulder, and ankle require large ranges of motion for human movement to occur efficiently.

Relative to the golf swing the mobility/stability pattern of human movement allows for the creation and transfer of energy through the kinetic chain from "feet to fingertips" into the golf club. If the mobility/stability pattern is dysfunctional relative to the golf swing, the development of speed will be limited, transfers of this speed to the golf ball will be compromised, and compensations in the golf swing will occur.

For example, if a golfer suffers from imited hip mobility. The ability to create an "X-Factor" in the backswing would be limited, and the initiation of the downswing by the hips would be negated. This would result in a loss of speed in the swing, an inefficient transfer of this speed to the golf club, and most likely the development of compensations in the biomechanics of the swing.

Mobility

The first pillar is mobility. Mobility is a combination of both joint range of motion and flexibility. Joint range of motion concerns itself with the actual articular structure of the joint (i.e. skeletal structures), and flexibility has to do with the extensibility of the soft tissues (muscles, tendons, ligaments) surrounding the joint. To better understand the relationship of joint range of motion and flexibility let's define both.

Flexibility can be defined as the optimal extensibility of all soft tissues surrounding a joint to allow for full range of motion. (Michael Clark, Director: National Academy of Sports Medicine) If certain muscles are "tight" or ligaments become "un-pliable" the ability for a joint to move through multiple ranges of motion may be hindered. Returning to our "limited hip mobility example", the golf swing requires the hip to be mobile in order to execute correctly. If the surrounding soft tissues (ligaments, muscles, tendons) are "tight" the hip will be immobile and unable to operate through the ranges of motion required too execute the golf swing correctly.

In addition to flexibility, range of motion is the second component of mobility. Mobility as stated above is the combination of normal joint range of motion and proper extensibility of the surrounding soft tissues. Range of motion is simply the number of degrees a joint should be able to flex, extend, or rotate. For example, the elbow joint is considered a hinge joint that only flexes and extends. The elbow joint should flex or extend a certain number of degrees. The hip and shoulder are ball and socket joints. These joint have large ranges of motion in multiple planes of motion. Limitations in the degrees of flexion and extension in the elbow or limitation in external or internal rotation in the hip/shoulder would be considered a limited range of motion in relation to these joints.

Mobility could be limited by a lack of extensibility by the surrounding soft tissues of a joint or the articular (i.e. skeletal) structures of the joint. For example, if the ankle joint were to have bone spurs, mobility in this joint would be limited not from the soft tissues surrounding the joint, but rather the articular components of the joint. Typically, mobility issues for the golfer are a result of soft tissue extensibility issues rather than joint range of motion.

Neuromuscular Efficiency

The second "physical pillar" is neuromuscular efficiency, which is often referred to as balance. It is defined as the ability of the neuromuscular system (nervous and muscular systems) to maintain the proper alignment, center of gravity, and coordinate the body during biomechanical movement. (Gray Cook, Athletic Body in

Balance, 34) Throughout the entire golf swing, it is necessary for the golfer to maintain the proper spine angle, create a weight transfer, and coordinate muscular movements. To perform this properly, you must be able to maintain balance of the body as a unit and control your extremities (i.e. arms and legs).

Neuromuscular efficiency within the golf swing is a responsibility of both the body and the mechanics of your golf swing. Improvement of your neuromuscular efficiency capacities on the "physical side of the equation" will allow your body to maintain the anatomical positions, coordinate movement, create a weight transfer, and control extremity movements within the golf swing.

Stability

Stability is the third pillar of our five pillars. Stability can be defined as the ability of any system to remain unchanged or aligned in the presence of outside forces (Greg Rose, Titleist Performance Institute Manual, 86) The development of stability within the neuromuscular system is contingent upon muscular strength. Strength is defined as the ability of your body to exert the required levels of force to perform the functional movement at hand. (Michael Clark, Integrated Training for the New Millennium, 369)

Stabilization in the golf swing is contingent upon muscular strength, and in order to execute every phase of the golf swing efficiently and effectively, a certain level of muscular strength is required. This allows your body to correctly sequence the muscular contractions required of the swing, maintain your spine angle, generate speed, and transfer speed to the golf club.

If we refer back to the mobility/stability pattern of human movement we can see what segments of the body require the development of strength for execution of a proficient golf swing. A quick review will indicate stabilization is required in the lumbo-pelvic-hip complex (i.e. core), lower extremities, posterior/anterior chain of the upper body, and scapular region of the kinetic chain.

Endurance

The fourth pillar of your golf fitness program is muscular endurance. Muscular endurance is the ability of a muscle(s) to repeatedly perform a physical action over an extended period of time without fatigue. Performing repeated physical actions such as the golf swing causes fatigue within the muscular system. As a result, muscular performance can decrease. Once this occurs the ability to swing the club efficiently is compromised. Endurance as with muscular strength can be a problem for the golfer. If muscular endurance capacities are poor, the ability to execute a proficient swing for an entire round can be challenging. The end result of such a situation is decreased levels of performance and an increase in potential injury. To prevent such a situations from occurring during a round or extended practice sessions, it is necessary to develop muscular endurance.

Power

Muscular power is the final physical pillar, and potentially the most important for optimal performance on the course. Muscular power can be defined as the ability of the body to create the greatest amount of force in a short amount of time. (Vladimir Zatsiorsky, Professor Department of Exercise and Sport Science, Pennsylvania State University) Basically, power is one component of developing speed in the golf swing. Power development on the "physical side" of the golf swing is a total body endeavor, meaning power generation in the golf swing is contingent upon the lower body, core, and upper body.

As a result of power being a "total body feet to fingertips action" in the golf swing, power exercises developing the entire kinetic chain are required. In order to develop the power outputs of your body, it is necessary to implement specialized exercises. These types of exercises will enhance the ability of your neuromuscular system to develop power, which in turn, as stated above, will enhance the amount of speed generated in the golf swing.

Summary

Mobility, neuromuscular efficiency, stability, endurance, and power comprise the "five physical pillars" of the golf swing. The "five physical pillars" of the golf swing support the mobility/stability pattern of human movement. Development of these five pillars is necessary to execute the biomechanics of the golf swing correctly, generate speed, and provide you the opportunity to improve your game. Inefficiencies in any one or all five of these categories will directly affect the execution of the golf swing, your performance on the course, and increase the chance of injury.

Chapter Three

Training Principles

The golf swing is a total body athletic action requiring the utilization of the entire kinetic chain "feet to fingertips" to execute a proficient golf swing. As a result, it is necessary for a golf specific strength and conditioning program to adhere to certain training principles. Adherence to these training principles will allow your training program to develop the kinetic chain specifically to the requirements of the golf swing and provide you the greatest opportunity for success on the course.

The following information will assist in developing your body around the requirements of the golf swing. Keep in mind when reading these principles they all cohesively work together to benefit your golf fitness program. The training principles we will discuss in this chapter are multi-planar, cross-specificity, limits of stability, SAID, individualization, adaptation, overload, progression, functional, and periodization.

Multi-Planar Training

The golf swing is multi-directional and multi-planar athletic action. As a result it is necessary for the golfer athlete to utilize an integrated training approach incorporating all three planes of motion (Sagittal, Frontal, Transverse). Training modalities developing flexibility, stability, balance, strength, endurance, and power in multiple planes of movement is required for optimal golf performance. All to often a general health and fitness program trains the body in one plane only. This is very counterproductive to the golfer as this type of training system does not address the physical requirements of the golf swing proficiently.

Sagittal Plane

The sagittal plane is an imaginary axis dividing the anatomical body into left and right sections.

Frontal Plane (Coronal)

The frontal or coronal plane is an imaginary axis dividing the anatomical body into anterior and posterior sections.

Transverse Plane

The transverse plane is an imaginary axis dividing the anatomical body into lower and upper sections. Rotary movements incorporate the transverse plane.

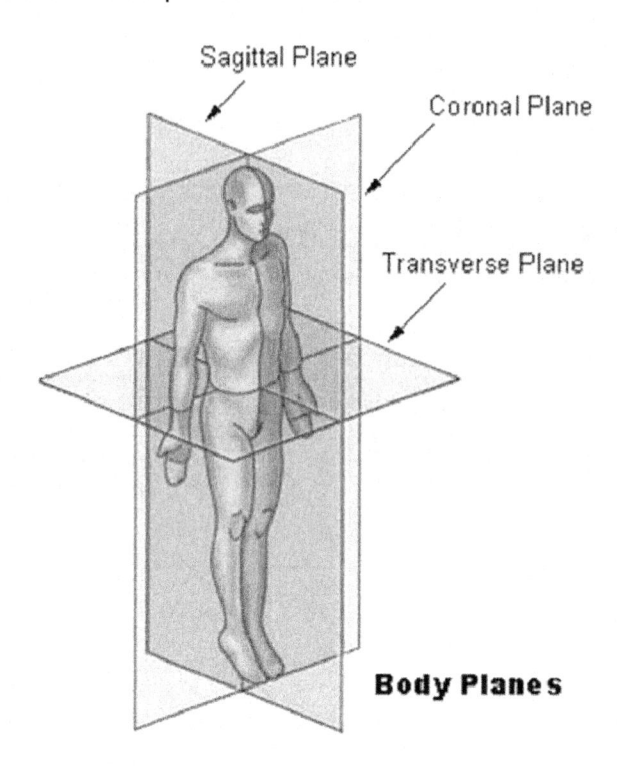

Body Planes

Cross-specificity

Cross-specificity is a reference to the similarities between a training program, exercises, and modalities relative to your chosen sport. In order to develop your body around the requirements of the golf swing: you must choose exercises simulating the biomechanics of the swing, utilize training modalities developing the mobility/stability pattern of human movement, and develop the physical requirements associated with the golf swing.

For example, during the backswing, rotation occurs in the core section of the body. In order for your body to execute this portion of the swing more effectively and efficiently, you need develop to develop mobility in the hips and stability in the lumbar spine. Such a task can be accomplished through cross-specific training defined as the training of the body to the anatomical positions, movements, and physical requirements of the athlete's chosen sport. (Carlos Santana, Director, Institute of Human Performance) This type of program is the foundation for the development of flexibility, balance, strength, endurance, and power around the golf swing.

The implementation of a cross-specific training program creates a transfer-of-training effect into your golf swing. A transfer-of-training effect is the ability of a training program to have a direct benefit on the performance of the athlete during competition. (Juan Carlos Santana, Institute of Performance, Boca Raton, FL) To better understand this concept let us use the example of a marathon runner and interior lineman in American football. The marathon runner and lineman are required to train extensively to perform in demanding environments. Both athletes spend many hours training for the rigors of either a marathon or professional football season. Now, consider what would happen if each were to trade training programs. Both athletes in all likelihood would perform poorly in their chosen sport. Why is this case? The demands placed upon the body by each of these sports are different and thus requires a strength and conditioning program specific to the physical needs of the sport. Golf is no different and for this reason it is imperative to utilize the principle of cross-specificity.

Limits of Stability

Limit of stability is the distance outside one's base of support they can go without losing control of the kinetic chain. Limits of stability is an integral component in the development of one's balance capacities for the golf swing. A centerpiece of the golf swing is maintaining one's center of gravity throughout every phase of the golf swing. Developing one's balance capacities via the process challenging your individual limits of stability assists in this process.

Adaptation

The ability of the body to adapt to the demands placed upon it by external stimuli is the principle of adaptation. All forms of fitness training are based upon this principle. For your body to improve its strength, balance, endurance, power, or flexibility, an external stimuli beyond your normal activity levels must be provided. For example, when you continue to perform flexibility exercises for the hips, strength exercises for the core, or power exercises for the legs your body will adapt by becoming more flexible, stronger, and powerful. To develop the physical pillars of your golf swing you must provide a stimulus in the form of exercise to create the necessary adaptation.

Overload

The overload principle states the human body will adapt to the increased resistance placed upon it by becoming stronger, faster, or more flexible. To improve your flexibility, balance, strength, endurance, or power you need to continually stress your body beyond what it has experienced in the past. For example, to constantly improve the strength within your lower body, increasing the load (weight) of your lower body resistance training exercises would create an overload on the body. Relative to strength development and overload, it is often thought the only way to overload the neuromuscular systems is through the utilization of dumbbells and barbells (i.e. weight training). This is untrue and the process by which the golfer will overload the neuromuscular system for gains in flexibility, strength, and power will be covered in later chapters.

Remember, for any physical improvement it is necessary to place an overload on your muscular system, and that overload may take the form of many different methods of training outside of the dumbbells and barbells. The next principle, progression, describes how to utilize the overload principle in relation to the principle of adaptation.

Progression

Progression is the implementation of exercises that progressively force the muscular and nervous systems of the body to work harder. In turn, this places an overload on these systems forcing the body to adapt over time. For example, if you started to perform a standard bicep curl with 10 lb. dumbbells for 15 repetitions, the exercise would be difficult at first. The reason for the difficulty is the curling action with 10 lbs. is above and beyond what your muscles are accustomed too (i.e. overload). Over time your body would adapt to the 10 lb.

dumbbells (principle of adaptation) and if your desire was to continue to get stronger biceps, it would be necessary to progress (principle of progression) to a more challenging weight or exercise.

This is a simple example of the principle of progression at work. Progressions of cross-specific exercise for golf follow some simple guidelines: begin with static exercises (stationary) and progress to dynamic (moving); begin with slow exercise movements and advance to fast; start with exercises in a stable environment and move to an unstable training environment, progress from bilateral extremity exercises to unilateral; commence with low force output exercises and progress to high output.

A sample progression for a golfer implementing resistance training for the lower body could be as follows:

1. Stationary two-legged body weight squat – progression number one: Jefferson squat– progression number two: goblet squat

2. Hip hinge – progression number one: two-legged medicine ball dead lift – progression number two: single leg medicine ball dead lift

This is a simple progression of both lower body hip and knee dominant exercises, and as you can see the exercises progressively overload the neuromuscular system as the body adapts.

SAID Principle (Specific Adaptations to Imposed Demands)

The kinetic chain (i.e. body) will adapt specifically to the demands place upon by external stimuli. External stimuli relative to resistance training can be in the form of load, volume, duration, or frequency. For example, if a golfer lifts heavy weights to improve lower body strength. The SAID principle indicates the neuromuscular system of the lower body will adapt to the heavy weights through improved muscular strength. It is important to recognize the SAID Principle relative to strength and conditioning programs for golf for the following reason; Often times an individual will perform the same training program over an extended period of time. Such situations negate the benefits of the training as the SAID Principle has become irrelevant and adaptation by the kinetic chain is limited.

Functional

Functional is a word that is almost overused in the field of strength and conditioning in this day and age, but it still has a great amount of importance relative to performance training for a sport. Functional can be defined as the development of physical components of the body with the intent on improving the athlete within their chosen sport. Golf is no different. Training the golfer should utilize functional training modalities improving the flexibility, strength, power, and endurance of the golfer.

What we must also recognize are functional training modalities and programming address the body as a unit. We know the body works as a unit to create locomotion, perform athletic actions, and execute the golf swing. That being said, utilizing functional training modalities is ideal for the golfer as it addresses how the body operates in the execution of the golf swing.

Functional training modalities are characterized by exercises training the body in multiple planes of motion, requiring the muscles of the body to accelerate and decelerate movements in multiple planes of motion, and force the kinetic chain (i.e. body) to stabilize during these movement patterns.

Individualization

The development of functional training programs require consideration of your age, medical history, current or past injuries, training experience, capacity for work, recovery, structural integrity, and training goals. You will respond best to a training program that is developed specifically in accordance to your needs and goals.

It is extremely important for you to apply this principle into the development of your training program. All the variables mentioned above have a varying affect on what we can do on the fitness side of golf. For example, certain individuals may require more attention to hip mobility whereas others need to address core training to a greater degree. We can not implement a "cookie cutter" training program and expect results for everyone. Take the time to individualize your training program and address what you need physically to improve your golf game.

Periodization

Most athletes use what is called a periodization schedule to plan their training. Periodizaton is the cycling of loads, volumes, intensity, and exercises within a given time period. The time frame may be divided into days, weeks, months, or even years. The cycling allows for a systematic approach to achieving improvement in your flexibility, balance, strength, endurance, and power as well as prevents overtraining.

Professional golfers typically utilize a periodization program splitting the year into three separate time frames; off-season, in-season, pre-season. The off-season for the professional golfer will focus on developing increased levels of flexibility, balance, strength, endurance, and power for the upcoming season. The pre-season portion of the program will typically reduce the amount of physical training performed by the golfer to allow them the energy required for the increased practice time before the season. Lastly, the in-season portion will focus on keeping the golfer playing injury-free golf. The greatest difference between all three segments is the amount of work (i.e. volume) performed. Off-season golf programs are high volume, pre-season are moderate volume, and in-season programs are low volume workouts.

It is suggested the amateur, high school, and collegiate level player adhere to a periodization program. This provides the individual the opportunity to take segments of the year to address physical aspects of the game for long term improvements. A common stumbling block is playing year round with little time spent on the physical side of the game. This type of approach limits the physical foundation development within the player and can deter from long term development within the game.

Intensity, Load, Volume, Duration, Frequency

Intensity is the amount of work for a specific exercise, groups of exercises, or entire training program. Different intensity levels of training will cause differing adaptations within your neuromuscular system. For example, if you were to perform lunges using a repetition range of 15-20 per set with 10 lb. dumbbells, this would elicit an increase in the muscular endurance capacities of your lower body. If the decision was then made to increase the strength capacities of your lower body using this exercise, changes in the amount of weight and repetitions would be needed. You might decide to use 20 lb. dumbbells allowing you to complete 10 repetitions of this exercise. This would shift the adaptation of the muscles in your lower body from increased endurance to increased strength levels.

The four variables- load, volume, duration, and frequency can be modified as a group or individually to increase the intensity of your golf fitness workout. Let's take a close look at these variables for a better understanding.

Volume:

Volume is the total amount of work performed in a given exercise, exercises, or entire workout. It is usually equated by multiplying the load x repetitions. For example, a dumbbell lunge performed with 60 lb. dumbbells for 12 repetitions would equate to a training volume of 720 lbs. for the exercise.

Load:

Load refers to the amount of resistance utilized for a given exercise. Load can be equated in the form of body weight, elastic resistance, or in the form of external resistance such as weight vests, medicine balls, dumbbells, or barbells. Repetitions and load are often linked. High repetition exercises typically require lighter loads, whereas low repetition exercises utilize heavier loads.

Duration:

Duration is the amount of time between each exercise within a specific workout. This training variable is often confused with frequency. Duration is strictly the rest period between sets. Typically a decrease in rest periods between sets increases the intensity of the workout. For example, a decrease in the rest periods between two sets of body weight squats from 60 seconds down to 30 seconds would increase the intensity of the exercises simply because the body is not resting as much between sets.

Frequency:

Frequency is the number of training sessions in a specified time period. An increase in the number of training sessions within a set time period elicits a higher training intensity for the overall program. For example, increasing the number of workouts to four from three in a seven-day time frame increases the overall intensity of the training program.

Always remember this: the intensity levels of your training elicit different adaptations within your neuromuscular system. A few examples should give you a very good understanding of this concept. A golfer who needs increased muscular strength in his/her legs would use a moderate load, repetition range, and volume to achieve the training intensity to elicit such results. Another golfer interested in increasing the endurance levels of their lower body would use lighter loads, higher repetition ranges, and volumes to achieve the training intensity and desired result. See the table below for detailed information on training intensity and variables for a better understanding.

Table 1.2   Training Intensity and Training Variables

TRAINING TYPE	LOAD/INTENSITY	REPETITION	DURATION/FREQUENCY
STRENGTH	70-90%	4-10 PER SET	1-2 min. 2-4 TIMES PER WEEK
ENDURANCE	70% <	15-25 PER SET	30 s. 2-4 TIMES PER WEEK
POWER	90%>	6 < PER SET	2-3 min. 2-4 TIMES PER WEEK

Before moving on, it is necessary you understand how each training variable affects intensity levels and adaptations by your body. For a full understanding review the table above and the information in the previous chapter on muscular strength, endurance, and power.

Integrated Performance Training

The integrated performance paradigm from the National Academy of Sports Medicine states all movement patterns during athletic and functional activities incorporate a repetitive series of stretch-shortening cycles. Components incorporated within the integrated performance paradigm include eccentric deceleration, stabilization, and concentric acceleration of the kinetic chain.

Breaking this scientific definition down indicates the entire kinetic chain (i.e. body) is utilized to execute the golf swing. And in order to proficiently execute the athletic actions of golf swing the neural muscular system of the body is executing a series actions in a specific sequence with timing. In order for these aforementioned physical actions to occur efficiently the body must have specified levels of joint mobility, muscular flexibility, segmental stabilization, strength, endurance, and power.

As a result a comprehensive strength and conditioning program for golf must entail modalities and exercises to address all aspects of the kinetic chain required of the golf swing. This type of training program incorporates a template with segments addressing each aspect of the kinetic chain required in the execution of the golf swing. The segments comprising an integrated performance training template for golf are as follows: 1) Mobility/Flexibility, 2) Corrective Exercise/Dynamic Warm Up, 3) Balance Training, 4) Core Stabilization, 5) Power Development, and 6) Functional Strength/Endurance Training.

Mobility/Flexibility

As stated previously, flexibility is the optimal extensibility of all soft tissues surrounding a joint to allow for a full range of motion. (Michal Clark, Director: National Academy of Sports Medicine) The process of improving flexibility and mobility for the golf swing occurs through a systematic approach incorporating a continuum of flexibility training modalities. The development of joint mobility and soft tissue extensibility requires the implementation of two different types of training modality. The first segment of training modalities referred to as self myofascial release exercises improve soft tissue quality and density. This is achieve via improvement in elasticity and viscosity in the fascial system and reduction in overactivity of the muscle spindles.

The second series of modalities incorporate static stretching exercises. These exercise improve soft tissue extensibility and assist in long term injury prevention. The processes by which static stretching exercises improve soft tissue extensibility is via the mechanisms of enhancing the plasticity and elasticity within soft tissues of the kinetic chain.

Corrective Exercise/Dynamic Warm Up

After the addressing one's joint mobility and soft tissue extensibility the next phase of your training template is corrective exercise and dynamic warm up. What you must recognize is due to our sedentary life styles, previous injuries, age, and the development of poor patterning our kinetic chain does not necessarily function optimally in terms of efficient movement patterns and muscular firing patterns.

For example, due to many individuals sedentary work environments where sitting at a computer is common, the ability of the kinetic chain to properly perform hip extension (i.e. hip hinge in the golf swing), and activate the glutes (glutes are a major power source in the golf swing) become limited. These types of situations severely limits our ability to perform complex athletic actions, create efficient movement patterns, and increase our overall athleticism. Not only does poor patterning and kinetic chain firing result in the aforementioned situations, the potential for injury increases exponentially due to inefficiencies present in our kinetic chain.

As a result of this situation a segment of your training template will be dedicated to the improvement of movement patterns, muscular firing patterns, and dynamic movement patterns. This segment of exercises will ingrain positive movement patterns into your system, improve muscular firing patterns, and prepare the body for exercise and athletic activities.

Balance Training

Balance defined is the ability of the body to maintain proper alignment, center of gravity, and coordinate the body during functional movement patterns. The process of developing the golfer's balance capacity entails utilizing one's limits of stability and challenging it with systematic and progressive series of training modalities. Balance training exercise will typically challenge your balance capacities through the process of maintaining balance in a proprioceptively enriched environment during the execution of corollary movements.

Power Training

Power in the most basic of formulas is strength plus speed. It is the combination of these two entities cohesively working together that allows for a sprinter to sprint fast, a pitcher to throw hard, and a golfer to swing with clubhead speed. Power in the golf swing is measured as clubhead speed, and a review of the kinematic sequence indicates clubhead speed is developed in stages. Speed development begins in the lower body, progresses to the core, and is completed in the upper body and hinging of the wrists.

In order for this segmental speed development to occur, the kinetic chain must have certain levels of strength as well as have the ability to generate speed. Speed development by the kinetic chain is contigent upon the neuromuscular system having the ability to generate force in the shortest amount of time possible. The process by which speed development can be improved with the kinetic chain is through the utilization of power exercises. These type of training modalities develop the explosive properties of the neuromuscular system via motor recruitment, CNS (central nervous system) functioning, neuromuscular synchronization, and rate of force production allowing for increases of speed during execution of the golf swing.

Core Training

The core is a reference to anatomical section of the kinetic chain consisting of the structures found within the lumbo-pelvic-hip complex. According the National Academy of Sports Medicine the core operates as an integrated functional unit providing intersegmental stability, deceleration, and acceleration. In addition, the core interconnects energy generated from the ground reaction forces of the lower extremities of the kinetic chain to upper extremities. The development of the core for optimal functioning encompasses a comprehensive, progressive, and systematic approach within an integrated strength and conditioning program.

The core is a highly addressed segment of the kinetic chain for the golfer athlete due to it's involvement in the athletic actions of the golf swing. Execution of the golf swing requires the maintaining of postural positioning, the generation of rotational speed, and the transfer of power from the ground reaction forces into the golf club. All of which require the recruitment of the core musculature to a very high degree. As a result for optimal performance and reduction of potential injury a comprehensive core program addressing the structures of the lumbo-pelvic-hip complex is necessary for the golfer athlete.

Strength Training

The kinetic chain operates as a unit producing force, reducing force, and transfering force efficiently. This allows for acceleration and deceleration of segments of the kinetic chain efficiently during functional and athletic orientated activities. The golf swing is no different, in that it requires the golfer to integrate the entire kinetic chain in the production, reduction, and direction of force. This allows for the efficient transfers of speed through the kinetic chain into the golf club. In order to achieve this requirement of the golf swing, specified levels of strength within the entire kinetic chain which can be developed through integrated, multi-planer, and multi-directional strength training modalities is required.

Summary

Let's put it all together so you feel comfortable before moving on. The training principles of multi-planar, cross-specificity, limits of stability, adaptation, overload, progression, SAID, functional, individualization, and periodization directly influence your training program. To improve your play on the course, match up the mechanics of the golf swing to the exercises in your training program (cross-specificity training). This allows for a transfer of training effect to occur within your game. Exercises that are functional are best for the golfer. The body adapts to stresses placed upon it, so for continual improvement the body requires overload of the neuromuscular system. It is best to utilize a systematic approach (progression) to achieve this goal.

Intensity is the amount of work performed in a given exercise, group of exercises, or entire workout. The intensity level of your training directly affects the adaptations by your body in the areas of muscular strength, endurance, and power. The training variables of load, volume, duration, and frequency directly affect the training intensity of your workout. These variables can be altered individually or as a group to elicit different outcomes from your workouts. Remember to be specific in terms of your training intensity to achieve the desired adaptations in your body.

An integrated training performance template is utilize to structure your program to address all physical aspects of the body required of the golf swing. Each segment within the training template will address specific components of kinetic chain required to improve performance and decrease the potential of injury. Golfers must pay strict attention to these training principles and adhere to the performance training template. As these principles and training template will allow you to develop the physical parameters of the body for the golf swing.

Integrated Performance Training Template for Golf

- Strength Training
- Core Training
- Power Training
- Balance Training
- Corrective Exercise/Dynamic Warm Up
- Mobility/Flexibility Training

Chapter Four

Assessment

An assessment involves a series of tests. The information gathered from these assessments will help determine the strengths and weaknesses of your physical makeup relative to the golf swing. Not only will these assessments provide relative information to for the improvement of your golf swing, they also function as a tool for the development of your golf fitness program, the setting of goals, and measuring results.

Fitness Assessment

The physical assessments in this chapter will provide you an abundance of information on where in the kinetic chain limitations affecting your golf swing are occurring. These assessments cover the categories of posture, flexibility, balance, muscular strength, endurance, and power. Guidelines for the tests are provided and it is strongly suggest you re-test yourself every 6-8 weeks to track your progress.

To ensure safety and reliability, each assessment should be performed with strict attention to proper execution. Follow the instructions for each of the tests and record your results. To provide you with the most accurate results, I recommend performing the tests in the order they are written.

Very little equipment is needed to complete these tests. Make use of a stopwatch, medicine ball (3-6 lbs.), and tape measure. Remember these tests in addition to determining the "weak links" in your golf swing, help you determine where to start your training programs, what areas to focus on in your program, and ultimately, the goals of your golf fitness program. Keeping a journal of all your tests results is also recommended. A journal allows you to review your tests to chart progress and set new goals. Now let's move onto the actual tests.

Assessment Procedures

Listed below are a series of tests to provide you with information on your posture, levels of flexibility, mobility, neuromuscular efficiency, strength, endurance, and power. Before performing any of these tests, be sure to be in good health and cleared by your personal physician. If you are uncomfortable or feel physically unable to perform a certain test, feel free to move onto the next one. For accuracy, perform each assessment 2-3 times, and in the order they are presented.

Postural Assessment

Poor posture leads to muscular imbalances, chronic injury, and the inability to maintain a fixed spine angle in the swing. It is of great importance to determine if postural deficiencies exist within your body. This will allow you to address this situation with the correct flexibility, mobility, balance, and strength training exercises. Listed below is a postural assessment to determine any mobility and stability limitations joint-by-joint in the body, beginning with the ankle, and progressing up the kinetic chain.

In addition to indicating any structural deficiencies, the static postural assessment will also provide insight into any muscular imbalances within the body. Golfers will often suffer from muscle imbalances where over development in one area of the body is causing dysfunction in another.

To perform this assessment correctly you will need a full-length mirror. Using an erasable marker or piece of tape, mark a vertical line directly in the middle of the mirror. Make sure the line covers the full length of the mirror and is straight.

Stand comfortably in front of the mirror at a distance where you can view your entire body. Align your body in the center of the mirror allowing the line on the mirror to dissect the middle of your body. Stand with feet slightly closer than shoulder width, hands resting at your sides, and eyes looking directly forward. This is the starting position of your static postural assessment.

The postural assessment will entail a visual observation of each joint in your body beginning with the ankle and working up the skeletal system to the shoulders. Each joint in your body, when viewed in the mirror, should be aligned straight with the mirror. For example the kneecap should point directly towards the mirror (internal or external rotation of the knee indicates a postural deficiency). In addition to joint alignment, observe each joint in relation to its opposing joint. For example, the right and left shoulders should be horizontally aligned. If the right shoulder is higher than the left this again is an indicator of muscular imbalances and joint restriction.

Listed in the table below are the visual cues to observe in each joint as you progress through the static postural assessment. Pay strict attention to each joint, stay relaxed, and utilize the information from this assessment to develop your golf fitness program.

Ankle	Internal Rotation (yes)	Tight Muscles – Adductors
		Weak Muscles – IT Band, Glute Medius, Glute Maximus
	Suggested Exercises	90/90 Hamstring, Bent Knee Back Hold

Ankle	External Rotation (yes)	Tight Muscles – IT Band, Glute Medius, Glute Maximus
	Suggested Exercises	Seated Hamstring Stretch w/ PB, Hip Circles
Knee	Internal Rotation (yes)	Tight Muscles – Adductors, Piriformis
		Weak Muscles - Glute Medius, Glute Maximus
	Suggested Exercises	90/90 Hamstring Stretch, Tubing Walks
Knee	External Rotation (yes)	Tight Muscles – IT Band, Glute Medius, Glute Maximus
		Weak Muscles – Adductors
	Suggested Exercises	Side Leg Raise - Adduction
Hip	Increased Extension (yes)	Tight Muscles – Erector Spinae
		Weak Muscles – Psoas, Abdominals
	Suggested Exercises	Cats Down, Cats Up, Crunch, Reverse Crunch
Hip	Increased Flexion (yes)	Tight Muscles - Rectus Abdominis
		Weak Muscles - Erector Spinae
	Suggested Exercises	Back Flexion w/ PB, Alternating Arm & Leg Extension
Shoulders	Internal Rotation (yes)	Tight Muscles - Pectoralis Major, Subscapularis
		Weak Muscles - Trapezius, Rhomboid
	Suggested Exercises	Chest Stretch w/ PB, Dumbbell Row
Shoulders	External Rotation (yes)	Tight Muscles – Trapezius, Latimus Dorsi
		Weak Muscles - Pectoralis Major
	Suggested Exercises	Lat Stretch w/ PB, Push Up

Mobility Assessment

A lack of joint mobility and soft tissue extensibility creates joint restrictions and the inability to draw the golf club through the required ranges of motion. The utilization of mobility assessments can assist in pinpointing muscles or joints that may be restricting your golf swing and causing compensations. Listed below are a series of assessments to assist in this process. Pay strict attention to technique when performing these assessments, be honest with your findings, and record your results.

Anterior Shoulder

Procedure

Lay flat on your back on the floor, knees bent, and hands resting at your sides.

Place hands behind your head and clasp fingers together.

Allow arms and elbows to relax.

Normal flexibility is when both elbows rest comfortably on the floor.

Standing Rotation Test

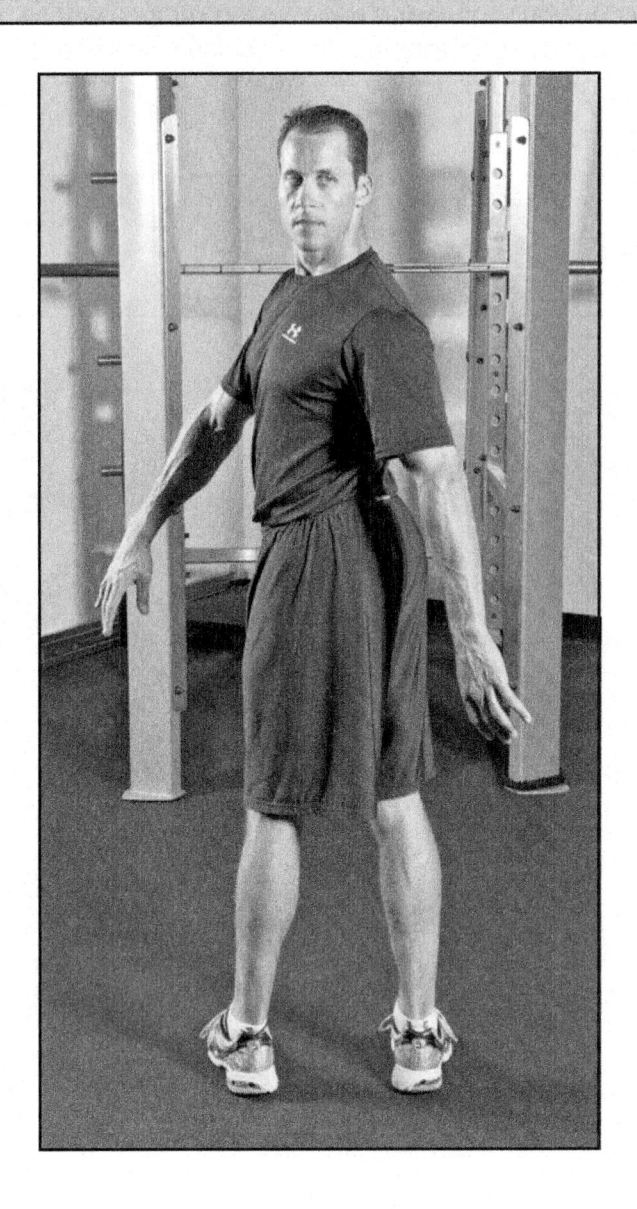

Procedure

Stand upright, feet slightly close than shoulder width, toes pointed forward, arms resting at sides, and back facing a mirror.

Keeping the feet in place slowly rotate to the right allowing the hips, torso, and shoulders to turn.

Rotate as far as possible allowing your head to face the mirror. Pause and obverse your hips and shoulders.

Normal rotation is when the hips are rotated approximately 45 degrees and the shoulders 90 degrees without discomfort or pain.

Repeat the rotation test to your left and again observe the amount of rotation in the hips and shoulders.

Shoulder Mobility Test

Procedure

Stand upright, hands on your hips, and eyes looking forward.

Reach over your right shoulder with the right arm.

Simultaneously reach behind your back with the left arm.

Attempt to touch the right and left thumbs together.

Repeat the test reaching the left arm over the left shoulder, and the right arm behind your back.

Normal flexibility of the shoulder capsule is when a "gap" of 4 inches or less exists between the thumbs in either position.

Lat Length Test

Procedure

Stand upright with back flat on a wall, hands on your hips, and eyes looking forward.

Simultaneously elevate both arms overhead, attempting to touch the wall with both thumbs.

Normal upper and mid-back flexibility is when the thumbs can touch the wall with the upper and mid-back maintaining contact with the wall.

Standing Toe Touch Test

Procedure

Stand upright with feet together, torso upright, eyes looking forward, arms overhead, and fingers together.

Slowly bend at the hips and lower the hands with the arms straight towards your toes.

Continue to bend forward at the hips keeping the knees straight.

Reach downward with the hands as far as possible trying to touch your fingers to the toes.

Normal flexibility is when the fingertips can touch the toes without the knees bending or discomfort in the lower back.

Prayer Position Test

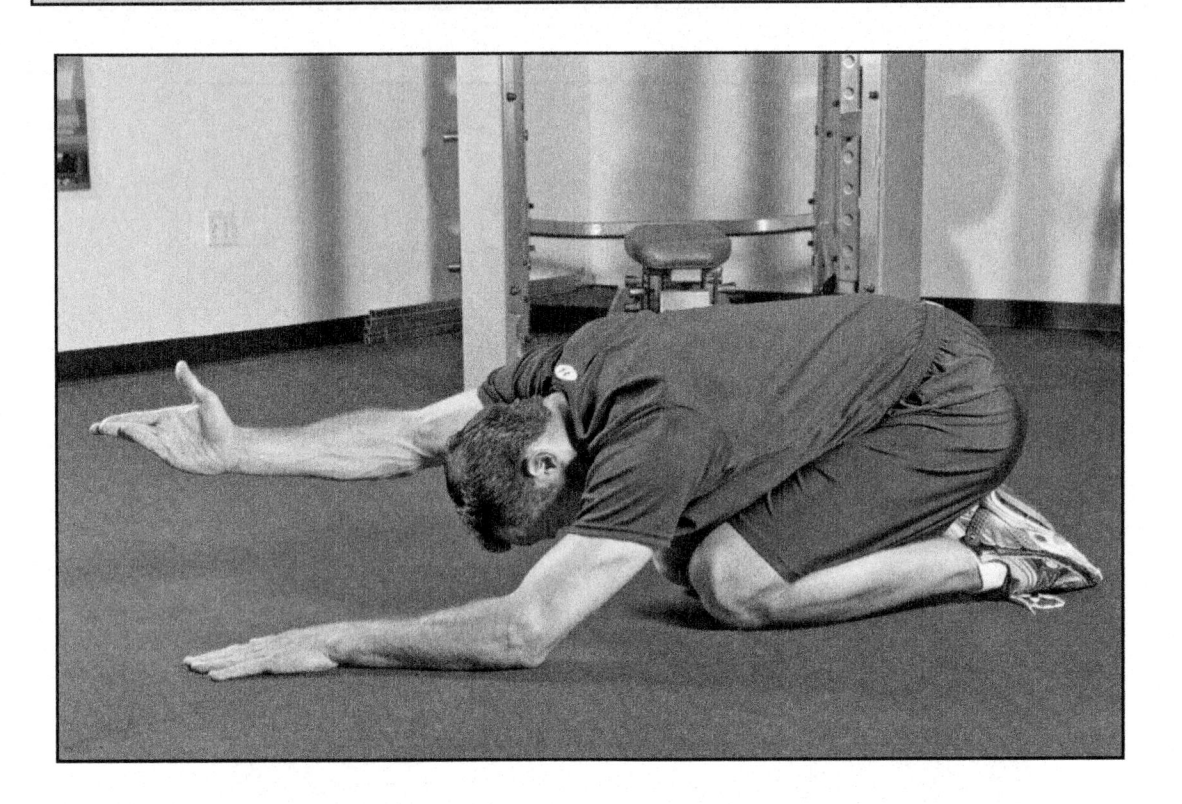

Procedure

Position both hands on the floor directly under the shoulders. Position both of your knees directly under the hips, eyes looking down and back flat.

Pull the hips backward towards the heels keeping the hands in place. Continue to pull the hips backward until the glutes are resting on your heels.

Rotate the palm of the left hand upward and attempt to elevate the hand off the floor while keeping the arm straight. Repeat the test with the right hand.

Normal mobility in the shoulder is when the hand can be elevated off the floor while the arm is straight and body remains in the "prayer position".

Balance

An assessment of your balance will indicate inefficiencies in the coordination of movement and potentially core stability issues affecting your golf swing. It is best to perform this assessment in front of a mirror. This will allow you to observe the execution of the assessment.

Single Leg Balance Test

Procedure

Stand upright in front of a mirror, feet slightly close than shoulder width, right hand on your hip, and left arm extended over head.

Begin by lifting the left foot off the floor and balancing on the right leg.

Proceed with this assessment by reaching the left hand down towards the right foot by hinging at the hip and keeping the right leg straight. Do not permit the left foot to touch the floor during the movement, and continue to reach the right hand towards the top of the left foot.

Return to the starting position and attempt to perform 10 repetitions of this assessment. Once complete repeat the assessment balancing on the left leg and reaching with the right arm.

Once complete on a scale of 1 to 10 (10 being the most difficult) determine the level of difficulty on the performance of this assessment and record your results. Pay attention to the ability to hinge at the hip while performing this assessment. A score of 1-3 is excellent, 3-5 good, above 5 less than average.

Stabilization Assessment

In order to execute a biomechanically efficient golf swing where the kinematic sequence remains intact, certain segments of the body must be stable. In addition, the ability to repeat the golf swing over an extended period of time requires muscular endurance. The assessments listed below will measure both your strength and endurance levels relative to the golf swing. Pay strict attention to technique during the execution of these assessments.

Bent Knee Back Hold Test

Use a stopwatch to time yourself.

Procedure

Lay with your back flat on the floor, knees bent, and feet together.

Elevate your hips off the floor inline with your knees and shoulders.

Do not arch the lower back or allow the hips to sag. Squeeze your glutes and hold this position.

Record the amount of time you can "hold" the correct position of the test.

A time of over 2 minutes is excellent, 90 seconds good, 60 seconds fair, less than 60 seconds poor.

Prone Hold Test

A stopwatch will be required for this test.

Procedure

Lay on your stomach with the elbows directly under the shoulders, forearms on the floor, legs extended, and your feet together.

Elevate your body into a standard push-up position.

Do not allow the hips to sag or elevate into the air.

Record the amount of time you can "hold" the correct position of the test.

A time of over 90 seconds is excellent, 60-90 seconds good, 45-60 seconds average, less than 45 seconds poor.

Functional Movement Assessment

The golf swing is a total body athletic action requiring the entire kinetic chain from "feet to fingertips" to be functioning properly for efficient execution. We know from previous chapters the body works in an alternating pattern of mobile joints and stable body segments. The functional movement assessments listed below will help determine if the body as a whole is operating as a "unit" to create movement. The functional movement tests will look at how your body is accelerating, decelerating, and stabilizing during multiple planes of motion. In addition these tests will assess bilateral mobility of the ankles, hips, and shoulders.

Multi-Direction Lunge Test

Procedure

Begin this assessment by placing pieces of tape in the fashion of a large clock face on the floor. Set a piece of tape at the 12, 3, 6, and 9 o'clock positions of the clock face and stand in the middle. Place the hands on your hips, feet together, torso upright, and eyes looking forward.

Proceed to step forward to the 12 o'clock position with the right leg into a lunge position. Pause for one second at the bottom position of the lunge, return to the center point of the clock and repeat the lunge to the 12 o'clock position with the left leg.

Once complete step laterally with the right leg towards the 3 o'clock position and perform a side lunge to the right. Pause for one second, return to the center point of the clock, and repeat a side lunge to the 9 o'clock position with the left leg.

Complete the assessment by stepping backwards into a lunge position with the right leg towards the 6 o'clock position of the clock. Pause for one second at the bottom position of the lunge. Return to the center position of the clock and repeat the backwards lunge with the left leg.

Once complete grade the level of difficulty of the assessment on a scale of 1 to 10 (10 being the most difficult). In addition record any difficulties in the completion of a lunge with either leg to any of the clock positions. A score of 1-3 is excellent, 3-5 average, 5 or above less than average.

Any differentiation between completion of the assessment by the left and right leg is an indicator of unilateral dysfunction in the kinetic chain.

Overhead Squat Test

Procedure

A dowel rod or similar object will be required for this assessment.

Begin in front of a full-length mirror, place the feet shoulder width apart, toes pointed straight, and hands grasping the dowel rod. Place the dowel rod on the top of your head and position the hands on the rod so that a 90-degree bend occurs in both elbows. Extend the arms straight overhead with the dowel round in-line with the head and over the feet.

Squat down as far as possible, keeping the dowel rod as high as possible overhead, pause for one second at the bottom position of your squat and return to the starting position of the assessment and repeat.

Discontinue the assessment if pain or discomfort is felt. Otherwise continue the assessment for a total of 10 repetitions. During the execution of the assessment, visually observe the ankle, knee, hips, torso, and shoulder joints.

A correctly executed overhead squat occurs when at the bottom of the squat: 1) the torso is upright and not leaning forward, 2) the arms are completely straight and dissecting the center line of body, 3) the upper leg is below parallel relative to the floor, 4) the knees are directly over the feet and not pressing outward or inward, 5) the feet are pointing forward and not flared outward, and 6) the heels are firmly on the floor.

Record the results of the assessment.

Utilize the information listed below to determine mobility and stability issues within the kinetic chain during the functional movement patterns of the overhead squat. A "yes" answer or "poor" marking points to a mobility or stability issue within the kinetic chain.

Table 1.3 Overhead Squat Assessment Chart

Ankle Range of Motion	Good	Poor
Knee Range of Motion	Good	Poor
Hip Range of Motion	Good	Poor
Shoulder Range of Motion	Good	Poor
Feet Rotate	Yes	No
Heels Elevate	Yes	No
Medial (Inward) or Lateral (Outward) Knee Tracking	Yes	No
Lower Back Arches or Rounds	Yes	No
Weight Shift Left or Right	Yes	No

Power

Power applied to the golf swing is measured by clubhead speed. The faster the clubhead is moving at impact, the farther a golf ball will travel. Power developed by the muscular system is one component of clubhead speed. An assessment of the power outputs by your body can help determine how to improve your clubhead speed. The assessments listed below will assist in determining your body's power outputs.

Jump Squat Test

Procedure

Begin by standing 4 to 6 inches away from a wall.

Place your feet shoulder width apart and arms overhead.

Begin the test by dropping down into a squat and explosively jumping as high as you can. At the highest point of your jump touch the wall.

Perform the test 3 times. Measure the distance from the floor to the point of your highest jump and record your results.

Overhead Medicine Ball Throw Test

A 4-6 pound medicine ball or similar object and a tape measure will be required for this assessment.

Procedure

Place yourself in a standard sit-up position (knees bent, feet flat, and lower back on the floor).

Grasp the medicine ball in your hands, overhead and resting on the floor.

Begin the test by performing an explosive sit up, throwing the ball forward over your knees.

Perform the test 3 times.

Measure the distance from your toes to the point where the medicine ball made contact with the floor, and record the distance.

Seated MB Throw Test

A 4-6 pound medicine ball or similar object and a tape measure will be required for this assessment.

Procedure

Sit on the floor, knees bent, feet together, toes pointed upward, and heels pressed into the floor. Grasp a medicine ball with both hands in front of your stomach.

Lean the upper body backward until your abs contract. Begin the assessment by rotating the torso as far as possible to the right. Pause at your farthest point of rotation for one second, and forcefully rotate towards the left releasing the medicine ball on the left side of your body.

Perform the test 3 times and measure the distance from your hips to the point where the medicine ball made contact with the floor, and record the distance.

Repeat the assessment to the opposite side of your body and again record your results.

Summary

Assessments provide you a valuable resource to understand and monitor your current levels of flexibility, balance, strength, endurance, and power as related to the golf swing. For accurate results, remember to take your time with the testing procedures. Keep in mind if you are uncomfortable in performing one of the above assessments feel free to move onto the next. The results of these tests will provide you with an excellent baseline of where to begin your training program, what areas of the body require attention, and what physical parameters necessitate development. Again, it is strongly suggested you re-test yourself every 6-8 weeks to track your progress.

Chapter Five

Mobility & Flexibility Exercise

The biomechanics of the golf swing require you to execute a series of biomechanical movements in a specific sequence. This in turn allows for the kinematic sequence of the swing to remain in tact, resulting in the generation of speed throughout the swing. Knowing this and how the body operates in an alternating pattern of mobile joints and stable body segments, we turn our attention to the concept of mobility and flexibility training.

The first step in the process of creating a foundation for the execution of the golf swing centers upon mobility. The process by which the development of mobility within the kinetic chain occurs is through the implementation of joint range of motion and flexibility modalities. The golfer athlete must understand it is not one type of training or group of exercises through which mobility in the golf swing is developed. It is through a comprehensive series of differing types of training modalities this goal is achieved.

Mobility and flexibility training consists of two types of modalities, self-myofascial release and static stretching. The goal of these modalities is improved extensibility of soft tissues associated with the muscular system of the kinetic chain. **Self-myofacial release** utilizes a bio-foam roller, stick, or therapy ball to apply pressure onto the muscular system of the kinetic chain whereas **static stretching** incorporates passive movement of a muscle to the first tissue tension point and holding it for a specified period of time.

Self-myofascial release addresses two components within the muscular system for improved extensibility. Research indicates that the application of concentrated pressure is influential on fascia in the muscular system. The pressure applied improves the extensibility and viscosity of the fascia located in the muscular system. In addition, self-myofascial release techniques reduce over activity within muscles spindles causing hyperactivity in associated soft tissues.

The process by which self-myofascial release is implemented is with the use of a bio-foam roll, stick, or therapy ball. The golfer athlete will roll over the target muscle searching for "hot spots" where tenderness or mild discomfort is felt. After you locate a trigger point (i.e. "hot spot"), maintain pressure on the spot for 10-20 seconds. The application of pressure for this period of time allows for an autogenic inhibition response within the muscle spindles and an elongation of fascia in the muscular system to occur.

Static stretching addresses extensibility within the muscular system of the kinetic chain through the process of taking the target muscle to its first tissue tension point and holding this position for 30 seconds. Research indicates the benefits provided by static stretching are in improved viscoelasticty in both the fascia and muscular systems. Recall from previous chapters, flexibility is the extensibility of all soft tissues in the body, allowing for the proper range of motion around all joints. The benefit flexibility training provides the golfer is through the elongation of soft tissues (muscles). Typically, certain muscles in the body are in a shortened position (i.e. "tight"), causing range of motion restrictions in their associated joints. The elongation (i.e. stretching) of these muscles through flexibility exercises will alleviate these restrictions allowing for proper ranges of motion to occur within the effected joints.

The order in which self myofascial release and static stretching is performed is of importance. Perform your self myofascial release exercises first and then progress to your static stretching. This sequence allows for the greatest benefit to occur to the fascia and soft tissue systems of the kinetic chain.

Mobility and Flexibility Exercises

Listed below is a series of self-myofascial release and static stretching exercises. The exercises focus on creating extensibility with the muscular system of the body for improved mobilty. Perform each of the self foam roller exercises for a series of 5 repetitions, addressing any "hot spots" with additional attention. The static stretches are to be performed in a passive manner, taking the target muscle(s) or joint through the suggested range of motion. In addition, pay strict attention to taking each exercise to the point of "tension" and holding the stretch for 30 seconds. Do not "bounce" during the execution of any exercise for this can result in injury. Technique is of the greatest importance with your flexibility exercises. Therefore pay strict attention to technique during the implementation of each exercise.

Calf Foam Roll

Goal: Decrease density of the calf musculature.

Starting Position: Place the foam roller on the Achilles section of your left leg. Extend the leftt leg straight, bend the right leg with the right foot flat on the floor, and hands next to your hips.

The Exercise: Slowly roll the foam roller up towards the knee. Press the left leg into the foam roll as you begin to move. Continue to move the foam roll over the entire calf and stop just below the back of the knee. Reverse the movement, and roll back towards the starting position of the exercise. Move up and down the calf of the right leg 3-5 times. Repeat the exercise with the right leg.

Tip: Discomfort will be felt in areas of the muscle that are "tight", when this occurs pause for 5-10 seconds on these "hot spots" in the muscle.

Hamstring Foam Roll

Goal: Decrease density of the hamstrings.

Starting Position: Place the foam roller under the knee of your left leg. Extend the left leg straight, bend the right leg with the right foot flat on the floor, and hands next to your hips.

The Exercise: Slowly roll the foam roller up towards the glutes. Press the left leg into the foam roll as you begin to move. Continue to move the foam roll over the entire hamstringand stop just below the insertion point of the glute. Reverse the movement, and roll back towards the starting position of the exercise. Move up and down the hamstring of the left leg 3-5 times. Repeat the exercise with the right leg.

Tip: Discomfort will be felt in areas of the muscle that are "tight", when this occurs pause for 5-10 seconds on these "hot spots" in the muscle.

Quadriceps Foam Roll

Goal: Improve pliability of the quadriceps and hip flexors.

Starting Position: Lay flat on the floor with the left knee bent at approximately 45 degrees. Place the foam roll parallel to your body on the front of the right leg just above the knee. Extend the right straight and place both hands on the floor above shoulder height.

The Exercise: Slowly roll moving the foam roll up the front of the right leg towards your hip. Continue to roll until the foam roll is resting on the hip, return to the starting position of the exercise and repeat 3-5 times. Perform the exercise sequence with the left leg.

Tip: Roll up and down the front of the leg focusing on the quadriceps and hip flexors.

Glute Foam Roll

Goal: Develop mobility in the hips.

Starting Position: Sit directly on top of the foam roll with your right glute in contact with the foam roll, bend the right leg, and place the right foot on the floor. Bend the left leg setting the left foot across your right thigh. Set both hands on the floor.

The Exercise: Sit your weight onto the foam roll through the right glute. Roll back and forth on the foam roll 3-5 times keeping the glute in contact with the foam roll. Again, sit on any "hot spots" for 5-10 seconds. Repeat the exercise with the left glute.

Tip: Rotate to your left and right to hit the entire glute.

IT Band Foam Roll

Goal: Improve pliability in the IT band.

Starting Position: Lay sideways with the right hip in contact with the foam roll. Extend the right leg straight, bend the left leg placing the left foot in front of the right knee. Place the right forearm on the floor with the elbow directly under your shoulder. Set the left hand on the floor in front of your chest.

The Exercise: Slowly roll down the side of the leg to your knee. Reverse direction and roll upward to the hip. Use the right forearm, left foot, and hand as the "driver" of the exercise. Roll back and forth on the IT Band 3-5 times. Pause on any tissue areas where discomfort is felt. Repeat the exercise on the left leg.

Tip: The IT Band tends to be "tight" on many individuals and as a result this exercise can cause discomfort. This discomfort should disperse after 2 weeks of foam rolling.

Adductors Foam Roll

Goal: Improve pliability of the adductors.

Starting Position: Lay flat on the floor with the left knee bent at approximately 45 degrees. Place the foam roll parallel to your body on the inside of the left leg just above the knee. Extend the right straight and place both hands on the floor above shoulder height.

The Exercise: Slowly roll laterally moving the foam roll on the inside of the left leg towards your hip. Continue to roll laterally until the foam roll is a few inches from the hip, return to the starting position of the exercise and repeat 3-5 times. Perform the exercise sequence with the right leg.

Tip: Roll laterally focusing on the inside of the leg to "hit" the adductors of the hip.

Thoracic Foam Roll

Goal: Improve density of the thoracic spine musculature.

Starting Position: Lay flat on your back, knees slightly closer than shoulder width, hands clasped behind your head, elbows next to the ears, and shoulders placed on the foam roll.

The Exercise: Slowly roll the foam roll down the upper back. Continue to roll until you reach the mid-point of the back. Reverse the exercise and roll upward to the shoulders. Alternate back and forth 3-5 times.

Tip: Keep the elbows next to your ears, and focus on the upper back.

Lat Foam Roll

Goal: Decrease density of the lats.

Starting Position: Lay on the right side of your body with the right arm extended straight. Place the foam roll directly under the shoulder joint of the right arm.

The Exercise: Slowly roll down the side of the body from the shoulder to the rib cage. Reverse the exercise movement back towards the shoulder joint and repeat 3-5 times. Repeat on the left side of your body.

Tip: Set your body weight into the foam roll and move slowly during the exercise.

Standing Calf Stretch

Goal: Improve flexibility in the calf musculature.

Starting Position: Place your hands on your hips, elbows bent, and body leaning forward. Extend your right leg backwards until it is straight, point your right heel forward, and bend the left leg.

The Exercise: Press your body weight forward by bending the left leg, keeping your right heel on the floor, and right leg straight. Continue to press forward until tension is felt in your right calf. Hold this position for 30 seconds and repeat with your left calf.

Tip: Keep your heel on the floor and back leg straight throughout the entire exercise.

90/90 Hamstring Stretch

Goal: Stretch the hamstring complex.

Starting Position: Lay flat on the floor, knees bent, and lower back pressed to the floor.

The Exercise: Grasp behind the left leg with both hands just above the knee. Pull the knee into your chest. Straighten the left leg to a position where a stretch is felt in the left hamstring. Hold this position for the 30 seconds and repeat the exercise sequence with your right leg.

Tip: Do not "bounce" during the stretch and gradually straighten your leg.

Piriformis Stretch

Goal: Improve flexibility in the Hips.

Starting Position: Lay on the floor, knees bent at 90 degrees, feet flat on the floor.

The Exercise: Slowly place the outside of your right ankle on the thigh of the left leg. Grasp the right ankle with your left hand and place the right hand on the inside of the right knee. Elevate the left leg to a position where the lower leg is parallel to the floor and the knee is bent at 90 degrees. If an additional stretch is required, simultaneously pull with the left hand and press with the right hand until a stretch is felt. Hold the stretch for 30 seconds and repeat with the opposite leg.

Tip: Maintain a 90-degree bend in the knee when elevating the leg.

Glute Stretch

Goal: Increase flexibility in the glutes.

Starting Position: Sit on the floor with the right leg in front of your body. Bend the right knee to 90 degrees while keeping the hips facing forward. Place the hands on the floor slightly in front of the hips.

The Exercise: Slowly press the upper torso forwards towards the right knee. Keep the hips facing forward. Continue to press the torso forward until a stretch is felt in the right glute. Hold this position for 30 seconds and repeat with the left leg.

Tip: Press the chest towards the knee and do not round the back during the exercise.

Kneeling Hip Flexor Stretch

Goal: Improve flexibility in the hip flexors.

Starting Position: Kneel with the right knee in contact with the floor. Place your hands on your hips, and bend the left knee at 90 degrees.

The Exercise: Begin by pressing the hips forward, allowing your left knee to bend. Continue pressing forward until a stretch is felt in the right hip. Once a stretch is felt in the right hip, extend the right arm overhead, and bend the torso to the left. Hold the stretch for 30 seconds and repeat with the opposite leg.

Tip: Keep your torso upright.

Cat In-the-Wheel

Goal: Improve flexibility in the lats and upper back.

Starting Position: Place both of your hands on the floor directly under the shoulders. Position both of your knees directly under the hips, eyes looking down and back flat.

The Exercise: Begin by extending your lower back upward towards the ceiling by lifting the hips. Continue to arch the lower back until it is rounded. Slowly pull your hips backwards towards the heels keeping the hands in place. Continue to pull the hips backwards until the glutes are resting on your heels. Hold this position for 30 seconds.

Tip: Keep the back rounded and hands in place throughout the entire exercise.

Seated Hamstring Stretch with Physio-Ball

Goal: Develop flexibility in the hamstrings.

Starting Position: Sit on top of ball, feet shoulder width, hands on hips, and torso upright.

The Exercise: Begin by extending the right leg straight, pointing the toe upward, and heel pressed into the floor. Slowly bend forward from the hips, pressing your chest towards the right knee. Continue to bend forward until a stretch is felt in the right hamstring. Hold this position for 30 seconds and repeat the exercise with your left leg.

Tip: Keep the torso upright and bend at the hips during the exercise.

Quadriceps Stretch with Physio-Ball

Goal: Stretch the quadriceps and hip flexors.

Starting Position: Place the right foot and ankle on the side of the ball with the right knee in contact with the floor. Set the left foot on the floor in front of the torso with the knee bent at 90 degrees. Lean forward with the upper body and place both hands on the floor.

The Exercise: Slowly elevate the torso upward placing the hands on your hips. Maintain position of the both the left and right knee on the floor during the elevation of the torso. A stretch will be felt in either the right hip flexors or quadriceps. Hold this position for 30 seconds and repeat with the opposite leg.

Tip: Keep the hips facing forward and the feet shoulder width apart.

Lat Stretch with Physio-Ball

Goal: Improve flexibility in the lats and upper back.

Starting Position: Kneel on the floor, physio-ball directly in front of you, and hands on top of the ball.

The Exercise: Roll the ball forward by extending the arms and allowing your hips to shift backwards. Continue to extend the arms forward and your hips backwards until a stretch is felt in the upper back, lats, or shoulders. Hold this position for 30 seconds.

Tip: Keep your lower back straight throughout the entire exercise.

Physio-Ball Chest Stretch

Goal: Improve flexibility in the anterior shoulder.

Starting Position: Kneel on the floor, physio-ball placed directly next to your left shoulder. Place the left arm on top of the ball with the elbow bent at 90 degrees.

The Exercise: Slowly lower your chest to the floor by bending the right arm. Continue to press the chest downward until a stretch is felt on the front side of your left shoulder or chest. Hold this position for 30 seconds and repeat with the opposite arm.

Tip: Align the elbow with the shoulder joint and progress slowly with the pressing of the chest to the floor.

Posterior Shoulder Capsule Stretch

Goal: Improve range of motion in the shoulder joint.

Starting Position: Lay with the right hip in contact with the floor, legs straight, and the right upper arm perpendicular to the shoulder capsule. Bend the right elbow to 90-degrees so that the right upper arm in resting on the floor.

The Exercise: While keeping the shoulder capsule and right upper arm on the floor, grasp your right wrist with the left hand. Slowly press the right forearm towards the floor. Continue to press the forearm down until a stretch is felt in the right shoulder and hold for 30 seconds. Discontinue immediately if a pinch is felt in the right shoulder, and do not allow the right shoulder to elevate or roll forward during the exercise. Repeat with the opposite arm.

Tip: Pay strict attention to technique with this exercise, go very slowly with the pressing of the forearm and do not aggressively press the forearm to the floor.

Side Lunge Stretch

Goal: Increase flexibility in the groin.

Starting Position: Place your feet in a wide stance with both feet facing forward. Place your hands on the floor directly in front of your torso.

The Exercise: Lean the upper body towards the left foot, bending the left knee, keeping the right leg straight, and both heels on the floor. Continue to bend the left knee until a stretch is felt on the inside of the right thigh. Hold this position for 30 seconds and repeat to the opposite side.

Tip: Keep your back flat throughout the entire exercise.

Summary

Ranges of motion for the golf swing are developed through a comprehensive series of functional training modalities. This process begins with self-myofascial release and static stretching exercise. Each type of modalities has a specific purpose in creating extensibility and the joint range of motion for you. Keep in mind the goal of flexibility and mobility training is the development of extensibility within the muscular system, and proper range of motion within the articular system through multiple planes of motion.

Sample Mobility & Flexibility Program

Exercise:	Sets:	Repetitions:
1. Calf Foam Roll	1	5
2. Hamstring Foam Roll	1	5
3. Glute Foam Roll	1	5
4. IT Band Foam Roll	1	5
5. Quadriceps Foam Roll	1	5
6. Standing Calf Stretch	1	30 second hold
7. 90/90 Hamstring Stretch	1	30 second hold
8. Piriformis Stretch	1	30 second hold
9. Keeling Hip Flexor Stretch	1	30 second hold
10. Lat Stretch w/ Physio-Ball	1	30 second hold
11. Chest Stretch w/ Physio-Ball	1	30 second hold
12. Side Lunge Stretch	1	30 second hold

Chapter Six

Corrective & Warm Up Exercises

After completion of your mobility and flexibility exercises the next building block in the equation is implementation of corrective and dynamic warm up exercises. As discussed previously for optimal performance of the kinetic chain daily and during execution of the golf swing requires optimal firing patterns within the kinetic chain. Due to previous injuries, lifestyles, and poor patterning the majority of individuals kinetic chain operates very inefficiently.

In order to reverse this trend, increase functioning within the kinetic chain, and provide you with the greatest opportunity to execute a proficient golf swing, exercises to correct these dysfunctions are required. Not only are corrective exercise required, a second series of exercises termed dynamic are needed to ingrain optimal firing patterns within the kinetic chain.

The corrective exercises provided in this chapter address the common dysfunctions associated with the majority of golfers. This would include glute activation, hip hinge mechanics, organization of the spine, activation of the core, and thoracic spine mobility.

The second series of exercises classified as dynamic warm up exercises are performed post corrective exercise with a focus on ingraining proper firing patterns within the kinetic chain from "feet to fingertips". These exercises are multi-joint, multi-planar, and required stabilization of the kinetic chain during total body movement patterns.

Corrective and dynamic exercises are to be performed post mobility training and prior to the commencement of the additional sections of your training programming. This section of the program typically requires 10-15 minutes to complete and is extremely important in the development of your body around the requirements of the golf swing.

Corrective and Dynamic Warm Up Exercises

Following is a list of corrective and dynamic warm up exercises that should be an integral part of your golf fitness program. These exercises are to be performed with strict attention to technique. The speed at which each exercise is performed is of less importance than completing the full range of motion which your body will allow.

Bent Knee Press Up

Goal: Activation of the glutes and deep stabilizers of the spine.

Starting Position: Lie with your back flat on the floor, knees bent, and feet together. Point your toes upward by pressing the heels into the floor. Elevate the right foot off the floor.

The Exercise: Elevate the hips off the floor by pressing through the left heel. Continue to elevate the hips until inline with the left knee and shoulders, pause for one second, and return to the starting position of the exercise. Repeat the "lift' of the hips. Perform 10 and repeat with the right foot in contact with the floor.

Tip: Engage the core throughout the entire exercise.

Flat Bench Hip Extension

Goal: Improve hip extension and activation of the posterior chain.

Starting Position: Place both of your hands on the floor directly under the shoulders. Position the hips in contact with the top of a flat bench, place both knees on the floor, eyes looking down to the floor and back flat.

The Exercise: Slowly press the right heel upwards, keep the knee bent and hips in contact with the bench. Continue to press the right heel upward until your right thigh is parallel to the bench. Pause briefly, return to the starting position and repeat for 10 repetitions. Repeat the exercise sequence with the left leg.

Tip: Keep the hips in contact with the bench throughout the entire exercise.

Alternating Arm and Leg Extension

Goal: Activation of core stabilizers.

Starting Position: Place both of your hands on the floor directly under the shoulders. Position both of your knees directly under the hips, eyes looking down, and back flat.

The Exercise: Simultaneously extend the left arm and right leg. Extend both the arm and leg until completely straight. Hold this position for one second and return to the starting position of the exercise. Repeat the exercise extending the opposite arm and leg. Alternate for 10 repetitions.

Tip: Maintain a "flat back" position during the entire exercise.

Windshield Wipers

Goal: Improve rotation in the hips.

Starting Position: Place yourself on the floor, back flat, knees bent at 90 degrees, hands between both knees, feet together, and head resting on the floor.

The Exercise: Slowly separate your feet keeping the knees bent at 90 degrees. Create the separation of the feet through rotation at the hip joint. Separate the feet as far as possible while keeping the knees and hands in contact with one another. Return to the starting position and repeat for 10 repetitions.

Tip: Keep the hands and knees in place throughout the entire rotation.

Thoracic Spine Openers

Goal: Improve upper body rotation.

Starting Position: Place your hands and knees on the floor with hands directly below the shoulders and hips above the knees. Place the left hand on the back of the neck. Press the hips backwards towards the heels while keeping the right hand firmly planted on the floor.

The Exercise: Begin by rotating the left elbow towards the right arm. Continue to rotate until the left elbow comes in contact with the right arm. Pause briefly and reverse the rotation towards your left. Rotate the left arm, shoulder, and chest towards your left as far as possible while keeping the left hand in solid contact with the neck. Pause briefly and repeat the exercise sequence for 10-15 repetitions. Repeat with the opposite arm.

Tip: Keep the hand in contact with the neck through the entire exercise.

Plank Scapular Push Up

Goal: Activation of scapula and protraction.

Starting Position: Lay on your stomach with the elbows directly under the shoulders, forearms on the floor, legs extended, and feet together.

The Exercise: Elevate your body into a standard push-up position. The hips should be directly in line with the shoulders and ankles. Do not allow the hips to sag or elevate up into the air. Hold the "push-up" position and "pinch" your shoulder blades together. Return to the starting position of the exercise and repeat for 8-15 repetitions.

Tip: Think about "pinching" a pencil between your shoulder blades.

Tubing Walks

Goal: Activation of glutes and abductors.

Starting Position: Place an elastic tubing loop around both legs just below the knees. Stand upright with knees slightly bent, feet shoulder width apart, torso upright, and hands on your hips.

The Exercise: Press the knees outward creating tension in the tubing. Hold this position throughout the entire exercise. Raise the left foot slightly off the floor and take a mini-step sideways to the left, keeping the right foot in place. Continue the exercise by taking a mini-step with the right foot towards the left. Alternate stepping left and right for 10-15 repetitions.

Tip: Keep the knees slightly bent and pressed outwards throughout the exercise.

Stork Turns

Goal: Improve hip mobility and separation between the upper and lower body.

Starting Position: Stand perpendicular to a wall, post, cable column, or golf club, feet closer than shoulder width, torso upright, and hands on wall. Hook the right foot behind the knee of the left leg.

The Exercise: Slowly rotate the hips left and right while keeping the shoulders parallel. Increase the speed of the hip rotation as you become comfortable with the exercise. Perform 10 repetitions and repeat the exercise with the left foot hooked behind the right knee.

Tip: Keep your foot planted firmly on the floor and shoulders stationary throughout the entire exercise.

Hip Hinges

Goal: Improve hip hinge mechanics.

Starting Position: Place a club in the middle of the back with the club head in contact with your head and grip on the lower back. Position the feet shoulder width apart.

The Exercise: While maintaining a flat back and the club in contact with both the lower back and head, slowly hinge at the hips, bend at the knees, and lower your free hand to a position slightly below the knees. Pause for one second, return to the starting position of the exercise and repeat for 10 repetitions.

Tip: Keep the club in contact with the lower back and head throughout the entire exercise.

Bent Knee Side-to-Side Leg Swings

Goal: Improve mobility in the ankle and hips.

Starting Position: Stand 6-10 inches away from a wall, post, or cable column with the feet shoulder width apart, toes pointed directly at the wall, legs straight, hips facing the wall, and hands planted firmly on the wall at shoulder height. Lift the left leg off the floor, placing the knee in-line with the left hip.

The Exercise: Begin rotating the right leg in a swinging motion in front of the body. Keep the knee elevated at hip height and swing the leg left and right as far as possible while keeping the right heel firmly planted on the floor. Perform 10-15 swings of the right leg and switch to the right.

Tip: Keep the heel on the floor throughout the entire exercise.

Straight Leg Side-to-Side Leg Swings

Goal: Improve mobility in the ankle and hips.

Starting Position: Stand 6-10 inches away from a wall, post, or cable column with the feet shoulder width apart, toes pointed directly at the wall, legs straight, hips facing the wall, and hands planted firmly on the wall at shoulder height. Lift the right leg off the floor.

The Exercise: Begin rotating the right leg in a swinging motion in front of the body. Keep the right leg straight and swing the leg left and right as far as possible while keeping the left heel on the floor. Perform 10 swings of the left leg and switch to the right.

Tip: Keep the heel on the floor throughout the entire exercise.

Straight Leg Swings Forward-Back

Goal: Improve hip mobility and flexibility of the hip flexors and hamstrings.

Starting Position: Standing perpendicular to a wall, post, or cable column, feet closer than shoulder width, torso upright, and left hand on the wall.

The Exercise: Lift the right leg a couple inches off the floor and begin to swing the leg forward and back, creating a pendulum motion. Swing the right leg forward and back as far as possible keeping the left heel on the floor and torso upright. Perform 10-15 repetitions and repeat with the left leg.

Tip: Keep your foot firmly planted on the floor throughout the exercise.

Sumo Squat

Goal: Improve squat mechanics and activation of entire kinetic chain.

Starting Position: Stand upright, feet slightly wider than shoulder width, torso upright, toes pointed forward, and hands on your hips.

The Exercise: Begin by slowing reaching the hands towards your feet attempting to keep the legs as straight as possible. Continue to reach downward with the arms and hook the hands under your toes. Once complete, begin lowering the hips to the floor between the legs. Squat down as low as possible keeping both heels on the floor. Pause for 1-2 seconds at your lowest position and extend the hips upward keeping the hands hooked under the toes. Once complete, stand upright, and repeat for 10 repetitions.

Tip: Keep the heels on the floor throughout the entire exercise.

Forward Lunge with Overhead Reach

Goal: Dynamically warm-up the lower body and improve mobility in the upper body.

Starting Position: Stand upright, feet together, arms resting at your sides, and eyes looking forward.

The Exercise: Step forward with the left foot into a lunge position. Plant the left leg on the floor, toes pointed forward, and torso upright, Lower your hips to the floor by bending both knees. Lower the hips to the floor until the left thigh is parallel to the floor. At the bottom position of the lunge elevate both arms overhead keeping the elbows straight. Pause for one second, lower the arms, and return to the starting position of the exercise. Repeat the exercise with the opposite leg. Alternate back and forth for 10-15 repetitions.

Tip: Keep the torso upright and extend the arms as high as possible overhead.

Side Lunge with Arm Extension

Goal: Dynamically warm up the lower body, activation of core, and thoracic spine.

Starting Position: Stand upright, feet together, arms resting at your sides, and eyes looking forward.

The Exercise: Lift the leg up bending at both the hip and knee. Step to your left with the left foot. Plant the left foot on the floor, toes pointed forward, and torso upright. Bend the left knee, keeping the right leg straight, and torso upright. Simultaneously elevate both arms forward to shoulder height keeping the elbows straight. Continue to bend the left knee until the upper thigh of the left leg is parallel to the floor. Pause for one, return to the starting position of the exercise, and repeat the lunge to your right. Alternate back and forth for 10-15 repetitions.

Tip: Keep the heels firmly planted on the floor and toes pointed forward throughout the exercise.

Spider

Goal: Warm-up the lower body and shoulders.

Starting Position: Stand upright, feet together, arms resting at your sides, and eyes looking forward.

The Exercise: Lift the leg up bending at both the hip and knee. Step to your left with the left foot. Plant the left foot on the floor, toes pointed forward, and torso upright. Bend the left knee, keeping the right leg straight, and torso upright. Simultaneously elevate both arms forward to shoulder height keeping the elbows straight. Continue to bend the left knee until the upper thigh of the left leg is parallel to the floor. Pause for one, return to the starting position of the exercise, and repeat the lunge to your right. Alternate back and forth for 10-15 repetitions.

Tip: Keep the heels firmly planted on the floor and toes pointed forward throughout the exercise.

Inch Worm

Goal: Dynamically warm up entire kinetic chain.

Starting Position: Position your body in a stand push up position, back flat, feet slightly closer than shoulder width, arms straight, and head a neutral position.

The Exercise: Slowly step the your feet forward towards your hands while keeping the legs straight. Do not bend the knees and continue to walk feet forward as far you can towards your hands. At your end range of motion pause briefly and walk your hands outward back into a push up position. Repeat the exercise sequence of walking feet forward and hands back to a push up position for 10 repetitions.

Tip: Keep the legs straight throughout the entire exercise.

Summary

Activation of the kinetic chain and ingraining proper patterning of movement patterns is essential. The utilization of corrective exercises in conjunction with dynamic warm up modalities accomplishes these two requirements of a comprehensive training program for the sport of golf. Execution of the corrective and dynamic warm up exercises are to follow your mobility and flexibility modalities in the training hierarchy.

Sample Pre-Round Dynamic Warm Up Program

Exercise:	Sets:	Repetitions:
1. Hp Hinges	1	10
2. Stork Turns	1	10
3. Bent Knee Side-to-Side Leg Swings	1	10
4. Straight Leg Side-to-Side Leg Swings	1	10
5. Straight Leg Swings Forward-Back	1	10
6. Sumo Squat	1	10

Chapter Seven

Balance Exercises

The ability to create neuromuscular efficiency is integral to a successful golf swing. Recall from chapter two balance is the ability of the neuromuscular system (nervous and muscular systems) to maintain the proper alignment, center of gravity, and coordinate the body during biomechanical movement. (Gray Cook, Athletic Body in Balance, 34) A golfer who lacks balance will often struggle with the golf swing, simply because they are unable to execute the movements of the golf swing correctly.

Neuromuscular efficiency exercises (i.e. balance training) are based upon the principle of challenging an individual's limits of stability (balance threshold). Limit of stability is the distance outside one's base of support they can go without losing control of the kinetic chain (Michael Clark, Integrated Training for the New Millennium, 174). For example, if you were to stand with both feet on the floor with your eyes open, this would appear very easy to accomplish. Now if you lifted your left foot off the floor and balanced on one leg, this would be more difficult because you are now beginning to challenge the limits of stability of your body.

Through this process of challenging your individual limits of stability, improvement in your proprioceptive qualities and kinesthetic awareness occurs. This in turns improves the ability of the neuromuscular system to maintain proper postural alignment of the body, maintain center of gravity, coordinate movements, and most importantly maintain balance in the golf swing.

Balance Exercises

Below is a series of balance exercises to assist in the development of the neuromuscular efficiency within your body. Many of these exercises will require you to balance on one foot or maintain a specific posture while performing a corollary movement. Secondly, you will notice the exercises will begin in stationary positions requiring you to balance on a single leg. The exercises will then progress with extremity movements creating a higher level of difficulty. Finally, exercises will be performed on an unstable surface increasing the level of difficulty. As a result, it is strongly recommended to perform only the exercises within this chapter that you are comfortable performing and can execute with proper technique.

Single Leg Balance Address Position

Goal: Improve balance capacities during rotational movement patterns

Starting Position: Place the body in a proper address position, knees slightly bent, fixed spine angle, arms crossed over your chest.

The Exercise: Raise the right foot slightly off the floor while maintaining your address position and fixed spine angle. Balance on the left leg in the address position for 30-60 seconds. Repeat the exercises balancing on your right leg.

Tip: Maintain a fixed spine angle throughout the exercise.

Single Leg Balance Golf Posture

Goal: Improve balance capacities within golf specific postures.

Starting Position: Place the body in a proper address position, knees slightly bent, fixed spine angle, and extend arms in front of body holding a five iron slightly off the floor.

The Exercise: Raise the right foot slightly off the floor while maintaining your address position, fixed spine angle, and arm position. Hold this position for 30-60 seconds and repeat balancing on the right leg.

Tip: Maintain a fixed spine angle throughout the exercise.

Single Leg Cone Reach

Goal: Improve neuromuscular coordination and lower body strength.

Starting Position: Place a towel, cone, or other object 2 to 3 feet in front of your feet. Place your feet together, hands on hips, and torso upright. Lift the leftt foot off the floor and balance on your right leg. Attempt to keep the left foot off the floor throughout the entire exercise.

The Exercise: Begin by reaching forward with the leftt hand towards the object in front of you, allowing the right knee to bend. Continue reaching until your hand is a couple inches above the object on the floor. Pause for one second at this point and return to an upright position maintaining your balance on the right leg. Perform 10-15 repetitions of the exercise and repeat on your opposite leg.

Tip: Stand upright between each repetition and allow the knee to bend during the exercise

Single Leg Toe Touch

Goal: Increase proprioceptive qualities of the body and improve the hip hinge.

Starting Position: Stand upright with your feet together and hands on your hips. Raise the left arm overhead and lift the left foot a couple inches off the floor.

The Exercise: Reach with your left hand down towards the right foot. Hinge at the hip to create the movement. Continue to reach downward to a point slightly in front of your right foot. Keep your left foot off the floor throughout the entire exercise. At the bottom position of the toe touch pause for one second and return to an upright position continuing to balance on your right foot. Perform 10-15 repetitions and repeat balancing on the opposite foot.

Tip: Maintain balance on one foot the entire exercise and return to an upright position each repetition.

Address Position Single Leg Rotations

Goal: Improve balance capacities during rotational movement patterns

Starting Position: Place the body in a proper address position, knees slightly bent, fixed spine angle, arms crossed over your chest.

The Exercise: Raise the right foot slightly off the floor while maintaining your address position and fixed spine angle. Begin to slowly rotate your shoulders to the right to the point of a complete shoulder turn. Return to the starting position of the exercise and repeat for 10-15 repetitions maintaining balance on the left foot. Repeat the exercise balancing on the left foot.

Tip: Maintain a fixed spine angle throughout the exercise.

Single Leg Golf Posture Swings

Goal: Improve balance capacities within golf specific postures and movement patterns.

Starting Position: Place the body in a proper address position, knees slightly bent, fixed spine angle, and extend arms in front of body holding a five iron slightly off the floor.

The Exercise: Raise the right foot slightly off the floor while maintaining your address position, fixed spine angle, and arm position. Slowly take a 3/4 quarters backswing, pause slightly at the top the backswing, execute a slow downswing movement keeping the club on plane. Return to the starting position of the exercise and repeat for 8-15 repetitions.

Tip: Maintain a fixed spine angle and the club on plane throughout the exercise.

Single Leg Airplane Rotations

Goal: Develop lower body strength and improve balance capacities during rotation.

Starting Position: Place feet together, bend at the hip so the back is flat, and chest is parallel to the floor. Extend your arms straight out from the shoulders, lift the right foot off the floor, extend the leg straight, and balance on your left foot. Keep the right leg straight and off the floor during the entire exercise.

The Exercise: Begin the exercise by rotating your left arm downwards toward the left foot. Simultaneously rotate the right arm upward. Create the rotation in the upper torso of the body. Continue to rotate to a position where the left hand is directly above your left foot, and the right hand is pointing straight up. Return to the starting position of the exercise, perform 10-15 repetitions, and repeat on the opposite leg.

Tip: Keep your chest parallel to the floor, and try to maintain your balance throughout the entire exercise.

Balance Pad Single Leg Address Position Hold

Goal: Improve balance capacities during rotational movement patterns

Starting Position: Position your left foot on top of a pad. Place the body in a proper address position, knees slightly bent, fixed spine angle, arms crossed over your chest.

The Exercise: Raise the right foot slightly off the floor while maintaining your address position and fixed spine angle. Balance on the left leg in the address position for 30-60 seconds. Repeat the exercises balancing on your right leg.

Tip: Maintain a fixed spine angle throughout the exercise.

Balance Pad Single Leg Golf Posture

Goal: Improve balance capacities during rotational movement patterns

Starting Position: Place the body in a proper address position, knees slightly bent, fixed spine angle, and arms extended holding a five iron in the middle of a balance pad.

The Exercise: Raise the right foot slightly off the balance pad while maintaining your address position, fixed spine angle, and club position. Hold this position for 30-60 seconds and repeat balancing on the right leg.

Tip: Maintain a fixed spine angle throughout the exercise.

Balance Pad Single Leg Cone Reach

Goal: Improve neuromuscular coordination and hip strength.

Starting Position: Place a towel, cone, or other object 2 to 3 feet in front of your feet. Place your feet together, hands on hips, torso upright, and standing in the middle of the balance pad. Lift the right foot off the balance pad, and balance on your left leg. Attempt to keep the right foot off the floor or balance board throughout the entire exercise.

The Exercise: Begin by reaching forward with the right hand towards the object in front of you, allowing the left knee to bend. Continue reaching until your hand is a couple inches above the object on the floor. Pause for one second at this point and return to an upright position maintaining your balance on the left leg. Perform 10-15 repetitions of the exercise and repeat on your opposite leg.

Tip: Stand upright between each repetition and allow the knee to bend during the exercise.

Balance Pad Single Leg Toe Touch

Goal: Increase proprioceptive qualities of the body and improve the hip hinge.

Starting Position: Stand upright with your feet together on the balance pad and hands on your hips. Raise the right arm overhead and lift the right foot a couple inches off the balance pad.

The Exercise: Reach with your right hand down towards the left foot. Hinge at the hip to create the movement. Continue to reach downward to a point slightly in front of your left foot. Keep your right foot off the balance pad throughout the entire exercise. At the bottom position of the toe touch pause for one second and return to an upright position continuing to balance on your left foot. Perform 10-15 repetitions and repeat balancing on the opposite foot.

Tip: Maintain balance on one foot the entire exercise and return to an upright position each repetition.

Balance Pad Single Leg Airplane Rotations

Goal: Develop lower body stability and improve balance capacities during rotation.

Starting Position: Place feet together on the balance pad, bend at the hip so the back is flat, and chest is parallel to the floor. Extend your arms straight out from the shoulders, lift the right foot off the balance pad, extend the leg straight, and balance on your left foot. Keep the right leg slightly bent and off the balance pad during the entire exercise.

The Exercise: Begin the exercise by rotating your left arm downwards toward the left foot. Simultaneously rotate the right arm upward. Create the rotation in the upper torso of the body. Continue to rotate to a position where the left hand is directly above your left foot, and the right hand is pointing straight up. Return to the starting position, perform for 10-15 repetitions, and repeat with the opposite leg.

Tip: Keep your chest parallel to the floor, and try to maintain your balance throughout the entire exercise.

Balance Pad Single Leg Golf Posture Swings

Goal: Improve balance capacities within golf specific postures and movement patterns.

Starting Position: Place the body in a proper address position, knees slightly bent, fixed spine angle, and extend arms in front of body holding a five iron slightly off the floor in the middle of a balance pad.

The Exercise: Raise the right foot slightly off the floor while maintaining your address position, fixed spine angle, and arm position. Slowly take a 3/4 quarters backswing, pause slightly at the top the backswing, execute a slow downswing movement keeping the club on plane. Return to the starting position of the exercise and repeat for 8-15 repetitions.

Tip: Maintain a fixed spine angle and the club on plane throughout the exercise.

Summary

Implementing balance exercises into your golf performance improvement program will improve the ability to maintain your spine angle and center of gravity during the golf swing. Recognize the goal of these exercises are to maintain postural positioning while executing corollary movements. Perform the exercises which you can execute safely and with a degree of proficiency. Utilize the progressions in terms of movement patterns and unstable surfaces to continually challenge your individual limits of stability.

Chapter Eight

Power Training

Power in the most basic of formulas is strength plus speed. It is the combination of these two entities cohesively working together that allows a sprinter to sprint fast, a pitcher to throw hard, a hitter to swing with power, and a golfer to swing with speed. The scientific definition of power states it is the ability to generate the greatest amount of force in a short amount of time. (Vladimir Zatsiorosky, Professor Department of Exercise and Sport Science, Pennsylvania State University)

Quite often when the topic of the golf swing driver in particular the word "power" is mentioned. You have probably heard the phrases "clubhead speed" and "ball speed". To understand the relation of power to golf, let us take a quick look at the swing.

When you are on the tee box with driver in hand, your goal is to impact the golf ball with a high level of force and hit it in the correct direction down the fairway. Impact with the golf ball occurs for a millisecond and research indicates the amount of time from address to impact is approximately one second.

Neuro-muscular power has a correlation to time. The definition of neuro-muscular power is the ability to generate the greatest amount of force in the least amount of time. Review of this definition will indicate immediately the need to train the parameter of neuro-musuclar power in relation to the golf swing. Power training emphasizes the ability of the kinetic chain to generate the greatest amount of force in the least amount of time possible. If you do not train the kinetic chain to develop the parameter of neuro-muscular power, then the ability to generate a large amount of force during your swing will be less than optimal.

In addition to driver on the tee box, power is a major contributor for your play from the fairway into the green. The greater speed at which the golf ball is impacted, the greater distance the ball will travel thus allowing you shorter irons into par 4's, and greater carry distance on your fairway woods.

Power Exercises

The golf swing is a total body "feet to fingertips" athletic activity requiring power generation from the entire kinetic chain. As a result the development of power for your golf swing will comprise exercises addressing the lower body, upper body, and rotary components of the kinetic chain. To take this concept a step further, lower body power will enhance your ability to generate ground reaction forces, upper body power will develop both "push" and "throw" power, and rotary power will enhance your transverse plane speed generation. The following power exercises are categorized into beginner, intermediate, and advanced. I recommend training approximately 6 to 8 weeks at each level before advancing to the next. The table below lists power drills in relation to the level of difficulty. Keep in mind the physical requirements (i.e. flexibility, balance, strength) needed before the implementation of these exercises. Perform your flexibility, mobility, warm up, and balance exercises prior to your power exercises. This will assure your body is prepared to execute the exercises in this segment of your training program.

Table 1.4 Power Drills

BEGINNER POWER DRILLS

- Kneeling Medicine Ball Side Throw
- Medicine Ball Power Drops
- Medicine Ball Overhead Throw
- Box Jump

INTERMEDIATE POWER DRILLS

- Front Twist Throw
- Medicine Ball Bent Over Chest Throw
- Overhead Stepping Medicine Ball Throw
- Squat Jump

ADVANCED POWER DRILLS

- Medicine Ball Side Throw
- Medicine Ball Chest Throw
- Overhead Medicine Ball Slam
- Single Leg Box Jump

Beginner Power Exercises

A series of beginner power exercises for golf are listed below. Keep in mind it is best to develop adequate levels of flexibility, balance, and strength before the implementation of these exercises. Adhere to proper technique with the execution of each exercise.

Kneeling Medicine Ball Side Throw

Goal: Increase rotary speed of the body.

Starting Position: Grasp a 3-8 lb. medicine ball in both hands. Kneel in a parallel body position 2-3 feet away from a concrete wall. Rotate the torso away from the wall and set the medicine ball next to hip furthest away from the wall.

The Exercise: Rotate the torso explosively towards the wall, keeping the elbows slightly bent. Release the medicine ball into the wall. Catch the medicine ball on the return from the wall, rotate to the starting position, and repeat the throw of the ball into the wall. Do not pause during the exercise, but rather use the body's stretch reflex and rotational capacities throughout the exercise. Perform 5-10 throws and repeat in the opposite direction.

Tip: Utilize the torso and hips in the exercise and keep the arms passive.

Medicine Ball Power Drops

Goal: Improve upper body push power.

Starting Position: Position yourself with your back on the floor and legs straight. Grasp a 4-8 lb. medicine ball with both hands at chest level.

The Exercise: Explosively extend the arms upward propelling the medicine ball into the air. Catch the medicine ball with both hands, return to the starting position of the exercise and repeat for 5-10 repetitions.

Tip: Propel the medicine ball upward with both arms providing equal amounts of force.

Medicine Ball Overhead Throw

Goal: Increase upper body throw power.

Starting Position: Stand facing a concrete wall. Place the feet 4-6 feet away from the wall, feet shoulder width apart, knees slightly bent, arms overhead, and grasping a 3-8 lb. medicine ball.

The Exercise: Bend the elbows and allow the medicine ball to move to a position behind your head. Allow the upper body to bend slightly backwards and then forcefully throw the medicine ball at the wall. Catch the medicine ball, return to the starting position of the exercise and repeat the throw for 5-10 repetitions.

Tip: Keep the feet firmly planted on the floor and allow to torso to bend forward during the throw.

Box Jump

Goal: Increase lower body power outputs

Starting Position: Stand upright in front of a 6, 12, or 18-inch step up box. Place the feet shoulder width apart and approximately 1-2 feet away from the box. Bend the knees slightly, torso upright, and arms resting at your sides.

The Exercise: Bend the knees slightly, extend the arms behind the torso, and jump up onto the box with both feet. Land softly onto the box by bending both knees during the landing of the jump. Step back down off the box and repeat. Perform 5-10 jumps and pay strict attention to technique.

Tip: Beginners use a lower height box and advance to a higher box as you become more comfortable with the exercise.

Intermediate Power Exercises

Advancement to the intermediate level power exercises will require approximately 6-8 weeks of consistent training at the beginner level. The exercises found at the intermediate level will require more effort from your body. Pay strict attention to technique and perform only the number of repetitions you can execute correctly of the intermediate power exercises. Again, it is best to perform 3-4 sets of each exercise two times per week.

Table 1.5 Intermediate Power Drills

EXERCISE	EQUIPMENT REQUIRED
FRONT TWIST THROW	4 - 10 b. Medicine Ball
MEDICINE BALL BENT OVER CHEST THROW	8 - 12 lb. Medicine Ball
OVERHEAD STEPPING MEDICINE BALL THROW	4 -10 lb. Medicine Ball
SQUAT JUMP	Body Weight - 10 lb. Weight Vest

Front Twist Throw

Goal: Increase rotary power.

Starting Position: Stand facing a concrete wall. Place the feet slightly wider than shoulder width apart and 2-3 feet away from the wall. Bend the knees slightly and grasp a 3-8 lb. medicine ball with both hands. Rotate the torso slightly and place the medicine next to the left hip.

The Exercise: Explosively throw the medicine ball towards the wall by rotating the torso. Aim the throw to a position directly in front of your torso. Maintain flex in the knees during the throw and generate the power from your hips. Catch the medicine off the wall and rotate the hips to your right. Continue to rotate until the medicine is directly next to the right hip and initiate the throw of the medicine ball back to the wall. Catch the ball return to the starting position of the exercise and repeat. Alternate throwing the ball from the left and right hip for 5-10 repetitions.

Tip: Maintain and upright torso and utilize the hips in the throw of the ball.

Medicine Ball Bent Over Chest Throw

Goal: Increase upper body push power.

Starting Position: Stand with feet shoulder width apart, hands grasping a 4-8 lb. medicine ball in front of your chest. Bend at the waist to a position where the chest is parallel to the floor, eyes looking down, and knees slightly bent.

The Exercise: Forcefully throw the medicine ball to the floor by extending both arms while maintaining the bent over position of the body. Allow the medicine ball to bounce off the floor, catch the medicine ball with both hands, and return to the starting position of the exercise. Repeat the throw of the medicine ball for 5-10 repetitions.

Tip: Maintain bent over position of the torso throughout the entire exercise.

Overhead Stepping Medicine Ball Throw

Goal: Improve upper body throw power.

Starting Position: Stand 6-8 feet away from a concrete wall or rebounder. Stand with the feet shoulder width apart, and knees slightly bent. Grasp a 3-8 lb. medicine ball and place your hands above the head.

The Exercise: Bend the elbows placing the medicine ball behind your head. Step forward with the left foot towards the wall and throw the medicine ball at the wall. Catch the medicine ball, return to the starting position of the exercise and repeat the throw by stepping forward with the right foot. Perform 5-10 repetitions of the exercise.

Tip: Allow to torso to bend forward during the throw.

Squat Jump

Goal: Increase power in the lower body.

Starting Position: Relax arms to your sides and place feet shoulder width apart. Point the toes slightly outward and keep the heels on the floor.

The Exercise: Lower the hips towards the floor. Bend the knees to do so. Continue to squat until the thighs are at least parallel to the floor. Simultaneously shift the arms behind your body. Explosively jump upward, extending the arms overhead. Land softly on the floor by bending the knees and hips. Reset to the starting position and repeat the jump. Perform 5-10 repetitions.

Tip: Increase difficulty of the exercise with the addition of a weight vest.

Advanced Power Exercises

Once you have demonstrated expertise within the intermediate level power exercises, it is time to progress to the advanced level. The advancement to the advanced level typically requires 6 – 8 weeks of consistent training with the exercises found within the intermediate level. It is best to perform 3-4 sets per exercise two times per week of the advanced level power exercises.

Table 1.6 Advanced Power Drills

EXERCISE	EQUIPMENT REQUIRED
MEDICINE BALL SIDE THROW	4-10 lb. Medicine Ball
MEDICINE BALL CHEST THROW	4-12 lb. Medicine Ball
OVERHEAD MEDICINE BALL SLAM	6-12 lb. Medicine Ball
SINGLE LEG BOX JUMP	BODY WEIGHT

Medicine Ball Side Throw

Goal: Increase rotary power.

Starting Position: Stand 3-4 feet away from a concrete wall. Stand with the feet shoulder width apart, and knees slightly bent. Grasp a 4-10 lb. medicine ball and place your hands next to the left hip.

The Exercise: Forcefully rotate your hips to the right, throwing the medicine ball against the wall. Allow the hips to rotate and your arms to fully extend. Catch the medicine ball and return to the starting position of the exercise. Do not pause during this exercise but utilize the body's stretch reflex during this exercise. Repeat the throw for 5-10 repetitions. Repeat the exercise sequence on the opposite side of your body.

Tip: Create a rhythm with the throwing and catching of the medicine ball.

Medicine Ball Chest Throw

Goal: Improve upper body push power.

Starting Position: Stand facing a concrete wall. Place the feet 2-3 feet away from the wall, feet shoulder width apart, knees slightly bent, and hands grasping a 4-12 lb. medicine ball. Place the medicine ball directly in front of the chest.

The Exercise: Forcefully extend both arms throwing the medicine ball against the wall. Maintain an upright torso and slight bend in the knees. Catch the ball off the wall, return to the starting position of the exercise and repeat. Perform 5-10 repetitions.

Tip: Keep the torso upright and forcefully extend the arms with each throw.

Overhead Medicine Ball Slam

Goal: Increase upper body throw power.

Starting Position: Stand with feet slightly wider than shoulder width apart, knees slightly bent, torso upright, arms in front of the hips, and hands grasping a medicine ball.

The Exercise: Squat downward by bending at the both the knees and the hips. Allow the medicine ball to drop in between the legs. Lower the hips until the upper thighs are parallel to the floor. Explosively extend the hips upward and simultaneously extend the arms overhead. Continue to extend the hips until the legs are straight and arms extended. Forcefully throw the medicine ball into the floor in front of hips using your entire body. Catch the medicine ball, return to the starting position of the exercise and repeat for 5-10 repetitions.

Tip: Utilize the hips in the throwing of the medicine ball downward.

Single Leg Box Jump

Goal: Increase unilateral lower body power outputs

Starting Position: Stand upright in front of a 6-12 inch step up box. Place the feet shoulder width apart and approximately 1-2 feet away from the box and balance on the left foot. Bend the left knee slightly, torso upright, and arms resting at your sides.

The Exercise: Squat downward on the left leg, extend the arms behind the torso, and jump up onto the box with the left foot. Land softly onto the box by bending the left knee during the landing of the jump. Step back down off the box and repeat. Perform 5-10 jumps with the left leg, and repeat with the right.

Tip: Pay strict attention to technique and land softly on the box.

Summary

This chapter has provided a series of power exercises. Remember it is crucial to develop a strong base of flexibility and strength within the body prior to the incorporation of these exercises into your golf fitness program. It is best to perform your power exercises 2-4 times per week depending upon your training program. Be sure to pay strict attention to technique in the execution of each power exercise.

Table 1.7 Sample Power Programs

BEGINNER PROGRAM

Monday:	Kneeling Medicine Ball Side Throw	2 sets x 8 repetitions
	Medicine Ball Power Drops	2 sets x 8 repetitions
Wednesday:	Box Jump	2 sets x 8 repetitions
	Overhead Medicine Ball Throw	2 sets x 8 repetitions
Friday:	Kneeling Medicine Ball Side Throw	2 sets x 8 repetitions
	Medicine Ball Power Drops	2 sets x 8 repetitions

INTERMEDIATE PROGRAM

Monday:	Front Twist Throw	2 sets x 8 repetitions
	Overhead Stepping Medicine Ball Throw	2 sets x 8 repetitions
	Squat Jumps	2 sets x 8 repetitions
Wednesday:	Bent Over Medicine Ball Throw	2 sets x 8 repetitions
Friday:	Front Twist Throw	2 sets x 8 repetitions
	Overhead Stepping Medicine Ball Throw	2 sets x 8 repetitions
	Squat Jumps	2 sets x 8 repetitions

ADVANCED PROGRAM

Monday:	Medicine Ball Side Throw	3 sets x 10 repetitions
	Medicine Ball Chest Throw	3 sets x 10 repetitions
Tuesday:	Medicine Ball Overhead Slam	3 sets x 10 repetitions
	Single Leg Box Jump	3 sets x 8 repetitions
Thursday:	Medicine Ball Side Throw	3 sets x 10 repetitions
	Medicine Ball Chest Throw	3 sets x 10 repetitions
Friday:	Medicine Ball Overhead Slam	3 sets x 10 repetitions
	Single Leg Box Jump	3 sets x 10 repetitions

Chapter Nine

Core Exercises

All golfers from the professional to recreational player must be aware of the necessity for certain segments of the body to be stable in order to execute the golf swing. Going back to our mobility/stability model of the kinetic chain, we are aware of the need to develop stability in the knee, pelvis/sacral/lumbar spine (hips/abdominals/lower back), scapular/thoracic spine (shoulder blades), cervical spine (neck), and elbow joints.

The development of stability within these joints/segments of the body allows a golfer to maintain a set spine angle, create rotary movement around this set spine angle, develop speed, and transfer this speed to the club. If an individual is lacking stability in any of these segments of the body, the ability to execute these components of the golf swing will be compromised.

As stated in chapter two, stability hinges upon the development of strength in the muscular system. In order to develop strength it is necessary to implement resistant training exercises into the your golf fitness program. Resistance training overloads the muscles of the body, and over time, results in increased levels of muscular strength and endurance.

The core is simply is a reference to an anatomical area of the body. The core is comprised of all neuromuscular structures from just above your knees to the upper torso. It includes all structures on the front, sides, and back of your body. Muscle groups included in the core are the glutes, hamstrings, abdominals, obliques, lower back musculature, and stabilizers of the scapula.

The core as a segment of the kinetic chain requires high levels of segmental stabilization in order to execute a proficient golf swing. This anatomical area is responsible for the maintenance of a fixed spine angle, the postural positions required throughout the golf swing, and the development of speed. In addition the core is the centerpiece of transferring speed developed by the lower body to the upper body during the swing. If the core is unstable and weak, the ability to transfer this speed will be less than optimal and lower power outputs will be the result. All that being said, the core is an extremely important section of the body for the execution of the golf swing.

Core Exercises

It is important to keep in mind the principle of progression during the implementation of torso stability exercises. As a result, I suggest beginning with bodyweight orientated exercises, progress to elastic tubing, cable, and physio-ball exercises. Following such a progression with your core exercises will provide the kinetic chain the appropriate levels of stimuli to continually get stronger and improve in terms of stability.

Bent Knee Back Hold

Goal: Develop postural strength in the lower back and posterior chain.

Starting Position: Lay with your back flat on the floor, knees bent, and feet together.

The Exercise: Elevate your hips off the floor inline with your knees and shoulders. Do not arch the lower back or allow the hips to sag. Squeeze your glutes and hold this position for 30-60 seconds.

Tip: Think about drawing a straight line from the shoulders to knees with your hips intersecting the line.

Prone Hold

Goal: Strengthen the abdominals and anterior of the core.

Starting Position: Lay on your stomach with the elbows directly under the shoulders, forearms on the floor, legs extended, and feet together.

The Exercise: Elevate your body into a standard push-up position. The hips should be directly in line with the shoulders and ankles. Do not allow the hips to sag or elevate up into the air. Hold the "push-up" position for 30-60 seconds.

Tip: Squeeze your glutes and think about your body being in a straight line from the shoulders to ankles.

Side Hold

Goal: Develop lateral stability of the core.

Starting Position: Begin on your right side, elbow directly under the right shoulder, forearm on the floor. Extend your legs straight with the left leg on top of your right. Do not permit your elbow to placed in front of behind the shoulder on this exercise, doing so may cause discomfort in the shoulder capsule.

The Exercise: Elevate your hips off the floor to a position in-line with the feet and shoulders. Hold this position for 30-60 seconds. Do not allow the hips to sag. Repeat on the opposite side.

Tip: Keep the arm extended and eyes looking at your hand throughout the exercise.

Physio-Ball Forearm Saws

Goal: Develop stabilization strength in the anterior core.

Starting Position: Position your forearms on top of the ball with the elbows bent. Position the body in a traditional plank position with the feet together, hips inline with the shoulders, and the back flat.

The Exercise: Slowly roll forearms forward away from the body as far as possible while maintaining a plank position. Return the forearms to the starting position of the exercise and repeat the movement for 10-15 repetitions.

Tip: Maintain the plank position of the body throughout the entire exercise.

Physio-Ball Table Top

Goal: Develop stabilization strength of the lower back, glutes, and hips.

Starting Position: Place the head and shoulders on top of the ball with feet shoulder width apart on the floor. Elevate the hips to a position horizontally in line with your knees and shoulders. Place your hands on both hips.

The Exercise: Extend the lower right leg outward from the knee. Continue to extend the lower leg until it is straight. Hold the extended position of the right leg for one second and return to your starting position. Repeat the exercise with the opposite leg. Alternate back and forth for 15-20 repetitions.

Tip: Keep the hips elevated throughout the entire exercise.

Physio-Ball Bent Knee Back Press

Goal: Increase strength in the glutes, hamstrings, and lower back.

Starting Position: Lie flat on the back and place your heels on top of a stability ball. Place the heels next to each other, bend the knees to 90 degrees, and extend your arms straight out from the shoulders.

The Exercise: Brace the core and extend the hips upward by pressing into the stability ball with your heels. Continue to press upward until the hips are in-line with the knees and your shoulders. Contract the glutes while pausing for one second at the top position of the exercise, return to the starting position, and repeat for 8-15 repetitions.

Tip: Squeeze the glutes at the top of the movement.

Cable Press Outs

Goal: Develop anti-rotational stabilization strength.

Starting Position: Grasp the handle of a cable or tubing with both hands at chest height. Position the feet perpendicular to the cable column and step 2-4 feet away from the column. Separate the feet slightly wider than shoulder width, square the hips, and shoulders so that they are perpendicular to the cable column attachment. Bend the elbows and position the hands directly in front of your sternum.

The Exercise: Press the hands directly outward from your sternum, do not allow the hips or shoulders to rotate during the pressing motion. Continue to press the hands outward until the arms are straight. Pause briefly and return to the starting position of the exercise. Repeat for 10-15 repetitions and repeat in the opposite direction.

Tip: Do not allow the hips or shoulders to rotate throughout the entire exercise.

Physio-Ball Circular Saws

Goal: Increase stabilization strength of anterior and lateral compartments of the core.

Starting Position: Position your body directly in front of the stability ball with both knees on the floor. Place the forearms on top of the stability ball with the elbows bent at 90 degrees. Elevate your body into a standard push-up position.

The Exercise: Slowly roll the forearms in a clockwise circular motion on the stability ball while maintaining a plank position with the body. Create as large of a circular motion with the elbows and forearms as possible. Perform 10-20 repetitions and repeat the exercise in a counterclockwise movement pattern.

Tip: Create as large a circle as possible with the forearms.

Physio-Ball Jack Knife

Goal: Create strength in the abdominals and postural muscles of the lower back.

Starting Position: Squat down and place your stomach on top of the physio-ball. Roll forward on the ball by walking your hands out into a push up position. Continue to roll forward until only the feet remain on top of the ball.

The Exercise: Hold the push up position and pull your knees in towards the chest. Continue to pull the knees forward as close as possible to your chest. Hold this position for one second, return to the starting position of the exercise and repeat for 10-15 repetitions.

Tip: Keep your back flat throughout the exercise and think of curling your knees in the chest.

Exercise Ball Leg Curl

Goal: Develop strength in the hamstrings and posterior chain.

Starting Position: Lay on the floor with the back flat. Place your feet on top of the stability ball, and arms extended to the side. Press the hips upward to a position in-line with the knees and shoulders.

The Exercise: Curl the heels inward towards the glutes by bending the knees. Continue to curl the heels inward as far as possible. Keep the hips elevated throughout the curling of the heels. Once the heels have reached your end range of motion, reverse the movement, returning the heels to the starting position of the exercise. Repeat the curling of the heels for 10-20 repetitions.

Tip: Keep the hips elevated.

Standing Cable Chops

Goal: Develop strength in the lateral compartment of the core.

Starting Position: Grasp the rope with both hands and step 2-4 feet away from the weight stack. Extend the arms straight and allow the torso to rotate towards the cable column. Place the feet slightly wider than shoulder width, knees bent, and torso upright.

The Exercise: Brace the core by contracting the abdominals, pull both arms into the chest and pause slightly. Rotate the entire torso from the hips up in the opposite direction. Allow your head to follow the rotation of the arms. Once completely rotated, press the arms downward away from the chest. Continue to press the arms downward until the elbows are straight. Return to the starting position, perform 8-15 repetitions and repeat the exercise in the opposite direction.

Tip: Maintain an upright torso throughout the exercise.

Standing Cable Lift

Goal: Increase diagonal strength in the torso.

Starting Position: Grasp the rope with both hands and step 2-4 feet away from the weight stack. Extend the arms straight and allow the torso to rotate towards the cable column. Place the feet slightly wider than shoulder width, knees bent, and torso upright.

The Exercise: Brace the core by contracting the abdominals, pull upward on the rope with both arms towards the chest, pause briefly, and rotate the entire torso from the hips in the opposite direction. Allow your head to follow the rotation of the chest. Once completely rotated, press the arms upward above the shoulders. Continue to press upward until the arms are straight. Return to the starting position of the exercise, perform 8-15 repetitions, and repeat the exercise in the opposite direction.

Tip: Allow the entire torso to rotate during the exercise.

Scapular Exercises

Recalling information from the beginning of this chapter we are aware the core encompasses structures from just above the knees to the upper torso. Developing stabilization in all the structures associated with the lumbo-pelvic-hip complex and scapula are necessary to create the required levels of segmental stabilization for the golf swing. As a result a series of elastic tubing exercises are provide to address the scapula region of the core for purposes of comprehensive stabilization within this segment of the kinetic chain.

Physio-Ball Y's

Goal: Develop stability in the scapula.

Starting Position: Lie on top of the physio-ball with your stomach on the ball. Legs straight, toes on the floor, chest off the ball, arms straight, and thumbs pointed upward.

The Exercise: Extend both arms simultaneously upward towards the ceiling. Keep the arms straight and the thumbs pointed upward. Continue to elevate the arms upward to head height, pause for one second, return to the starting position of the exercise and repeat for 8-15 repetitions.

Tip: Keep the thumbs pointed upward and arms straight.

Physio-Ball T's

Goal: Increase scapular stability of the torso.

Starting Position: Lie on top of the physio-ball with your stomach on the ball. Legs straight, toes on the floor, chest off the ball, arms straight out from the shoulders, and thumbs pointed out to the sides

The Exercises: Pinch the shoulder blades together and extend the arms out the sides. Continue to raise the arms until a "T" is formed with the torso. Keep the arms straight and pull the shoulders blades together. Return to the starting position of the exercise and repeat for 8-15 repetitions.

Tip: Attempt to squeeze the shoulder blades together during the exercise.

Physio-Ball W's

Goal: Improve scapular strength.

Starting Position: Lie on top of the physio-ball with your stomach on the ball. Legs straight, toes on the floor, chest off the ball, arms bent, elbows slightly in front of your chest, and thumbs pointed upward.

The Exercise: Elevate the elbows upward towards the ceiling squeezing the shoulder blades together. Pause for one second, return to the starting position, and repeat for 8-15 repetitions.

Tip: Visualize a reverse pec dec machine movement.

Physio-Ball L's

Goal: Increase shoulder stability.

Starting Position: Lie on top of the physio-ball with your stomach on the ball. Legs straight, toes on the floor, chest off the ball, arms bent at 90 degrees, and elbows directly inline with the shoulders.

The Exercise: Squeeze the shoulder blades together and simultaneously rotate both forearms upward towards the ceiling. Keep the elbows inline with the shoulders, and continue to rotate the forearms to head height. Pause for one second, return to the starting position of the exercise and repeat for 8-15 repetitions.

Tip: Do not allow the elbows to drop towards the floor during the exercise.

Summary

This chapter has outlined a series of core exercises. It is important to develop stabilization in the lumbo-pelvic-hip complex and scapular region of the core. This allows you the opportunity to maintain the postural positions of the swing, rotate around a fixed spine angle, reduce the potential for lower back injuries, and generate speed.

Table 1.8 Sample Core Programs

BEGINNER PROGRAM

Monday:	Bent Knee Back Hold	1 set x 30 seconds
	Prone Hold	1 set x 30 seconds
	Side Hold	1 set x 30 seconds
	Physio-Ball Y-T-W-L	1 set x 10 repetitions
Wednesday:	Bent Knee Back Hold	1 set x 30 seconds
	Prone Hold	1 set x 30 seconds
	Side Hold	1 set x 30 seconds
	Physio-Ball Y-T-W-L	1 set x 10 repetitions
Friday:	Bent Knee Back Hold	1 set x 30 seconds
	Prone Hold	1 set x 30 seconds
	Side Hold	1 set x 30 seconds
	Physio-Ball Y-T-W-L	1 set x 10 repetitions

INTERMEDIATE PROGRAM

Monday:	Physio-Ball Saws	2 sets x 15 repetitions
	Physio-Ball Table Top	2 sets x 15 repetitions
	Physio-Ball Y-T-W-L w/ 3 lb. dumbbells	1 set x 10 repetitions
Wednesday:	Physio-Ball Bent Knee Back Press	2 sets x 15 repetitions

	Standing Cable Press Outs	2 sets x 15 repetitions
	Physio-Ball Y-T-W-L w/ 3 lb. dumbbells	1 set x 10 repetitions
Friday:	Physio-Ball Saws	2 sets x 15 repetitions
	Physio-Ball Table Top	2 sets x 15 repetitions
	Physio-Ball Y-T-W-L w/ 3 lb. dumbbells	1 set x 10 repetitions

ADVANCED PROGRAM

Monday:	Physio-Ball Circular Saws	3 sets x 15 repetitions
	Physio-Ball Jack Knife	3 sets x 15 repetitions
	Physio-Ball Y-T-W-L w/ 5 lb. dumbbells	1 set x 12 repetitions
Tuesday:	Physio-Ball Leg Curls	3 sets x 15 repetitions
	Stabding Cable Chops/Lifts	3 sets x 15 repetitions
Thursday:	Physio-Ball Circular Saws	3 sets x 15 repetitions
	Physio-Ball Jack Knife	3 sets x 15 repetitions
	Physio-Ball Y-T-W-L w/ 5 lb. dumbbells	1 set x 12 repetitions
Friday:	Physio-Ball Leg Curls	3 sets x 15 repetitions
	Stabding Cable Chops/Lifts	3 sets x 15 repetitions

Chapter Ten

Functional Strength Exercises

Up to this point we have provided you with a number of principles applicable to a golf specific training program, and the exercises to improve your performance. Information on balance, stabilization, torso, and joint integrity training have been presented in the last couple of chapters. These previous chapters of information make up the foundation of your training program. If any of the above mentioned areas of training are ignored then the outcome of your entire program will be less than optimal. We now turn to the functional strength training section of your training program.

We have discussed the importance of the kinetic chain, functional exercises, and cross specificity training. This is the point in your training program again where these principles are essential. We know golf is a "feet to fingertip" sport, and every muscle in the kinetic chain is being utilized either concentrically, eccentrically, or isometrically to create the given athletic movement. We understand that for the optimal performance on the course our training modalities must mirror the neuromuscular actions during competition (i.e. cross specificity training). This information brings us to the point where we are concurrently. We have created the foundation of our training program with modalities agree with these principles, but now what do we do to incorporate exercises that train the larger muscles (i.e. prime movers) of the neuromuscular system of the body?

Remembering the manner in which we train them must be cross specific to the movement patterns associated with the golf swing. The above information should give you a pretty good clue. We need to train the kinetic chain of the body with multi-planar, multi-directional, isometric, concentric, and eccentric exercise. The exercises should focus on developing the neuromuscular capacities of endurance, strength, strength endurance, and power specific to the sport of golf. Specific to the sport of golf refers to training the body a unit, not in isolated muscle groups because we know that golf is a sport in which the entire neuromuscular system is used to swing the club. As a result of this information we will be developing movement patterns incorporating the entire kinetic chain. This chapter will provide you this knowledge and provide the correct resistance training exercises for golf.

During the implementation of functional strength exercises, it is extremely important to follow the principle of progression. As stated previously, many younger players are not physically ready to be challenged with external resistance exercises in the form of barbells and dumbbells. Implementation of such exercises before the athlete is physically ready will detract from performance and increase the possibility of injury.

As a result it is best to begin the younger ball player with body weight orientated functional exercises, and progress accordingly. Simple guidelines of progressions for functional strength training exercises are as follows:

1) Commence with body weight training and advance to externally loaded exercises.

2) Begin with static (stationary) exercises and progress to dynamic (moving) exercises.

3) Start with slow exercise movements and advance to fast.

4) Initiate training with bilateral (i.e. two-legged, two-arm) orientated exercises and progress to unilateral (i.e. one-legged, one arm, or alternating arm/leg) exercises.

Functional Strength Exercises

Functional strength exercises are best performed 2-4 times per week and after the warm-up, flexibility, balance, and torso stability sections of your program. Functional strength exercises cause extensive muscular fatigue. As a result, it is suggested not to perform functional strength exercises on consecutive days; rather, allow a recovery time of 48 to 72 hours for the body between such exercises.

In addition it is best to select a comprehensive set of exercises from this chapter requiring the body to push (i.e. lower body squatting and upper pressing), pull (i.e. lower body and upper body pulling), and rotate during a single workout or consecutive workouts. Sample programs found in later chapters to assist you in this process of selecting the correct exercises to achieve this goal.

Body Weight Squat

Goal: Increase lower body push strength in the hips, glutes, and lower body.

Starting Position: Clasp hands behind your head and place feet shoulder width apart. Point the toes slightly outward and keep the heels on the floor.

The Exercise: Slowly lower the hips in a controlled manner towards the floor. Bend the knees to do so. Continue to squat until the thighs are parallel to the floor. Hold the bottom position of the squat for one second and return to the starting position of the exercise. Repeat the squat for 8-15 repetitions.

Tip: Keep the heels on the floor throughout the squat.

Jefferson Squat

Goal: Increase push strength on the lower body,

Starting Position: Grasp a dumbbell with both hands in front the hips. Extend the arms straight, place the feet slightly wider than shoulder width apart, toes pointed outward at 45 degrees, and heels on the floor. Maintain an upright torso with the eyes looking forward, and arms extended straight.

The Exercise: Slowly lower the hips while keeping the torso upright by bending the knees. Continue to squat downward until the thighs are parallel to the floor. Pause for one second, return to the starting position of the exercise, and repeat for 8-15 repetitions.

Tip: Keep the torso upright and heels on the floor throughout the entire exercise.

Goblet Squat

Goal: Improve push strength in the lower body.

Starting Position: Grasp a dumbbell with both hands in front the chest. Rest the dumbbell in the palms of both hands, and elbows pointing down. Place the feet slightly wider than shoulder width apart, toes pointed outward at 45 degrees, and heels on the floor. Maintain an upright torso with the eyes looking forward, and arms extended straight.

The Exercise: Slowly lower the hips while keeping the torso upright by bending the knees. Continue to squat downward until the thighs are parallel to the floor. Pause for one second, return to the starting position of the exercise, and repeat for 8-15 repetitions.

Tip: Keep the torso upright and heels on the floor throughout the entire exercise.

Bulgarian Split Squat

Goal: Increase unilateral push strength in the hips, glutes, and lower body.

Starting Position: Place the left foot in front of the torso, knee slightly bent, and toes pointed forward. Set the right foot firmly on top of a step-up box or flat bench. Bend the right knee slightly, setting your body in a traditional lunge position. Clasp the hands behind your head, and set the torso upright with the eyes looking forward.

The Exercise: Set your core by contracting the abdominals, and descend the hips slowly towards the floor, bend both knees to do so. Continue to lower the hips towards the floor until the left thigh is parallel to the floor. Pause for one second and ascend slowly to the starting position of the exercise. Reset the bracing of the core and perform 8-15 repetitions of the exercise. Repeat the exercise sequence with the right leg forward and left foot on the box or bench.

Tip: Maintain an upright torso throughout the exercise.

Weighted Vest Bulgarian Split Squat

Goal: Develop unilateral push strength in the lower body.

Starting Position: Strap a weighted vest onto the torso. Place the left foot in front of the torso, knee slightly bent, and toes pointed forward. Set the right foot firmly on top of a step-up box or flat bench. Bend the right knee slightly, setting your body in a traditional lunge position. Clasp the hands behind your head, and set the torso upright with the eyes looking forward.

The Exercise: Set your core by contracting the abdominals, and descend the hips slowly towards the floor, bend both knees to do so. Continue to lower the hips towards the floor until the left thigh is parallel to the floor. Pause for one second and ascend slowly to the starting position of the exercise. Reset the bracing of the core and perform 8-15 repetitions of the exercise. Repeat the exercise sequence with the right leg forward and left foot on the box or bench.

Tip: Maintain an upright torso throughout the exercise and go to parallel with each repetition.

Dumbbell Bulgarian Split Squat

Goal: Increase single leg lower body strength.

Starting Position: Grasp dumbbells with both hands. Place the left foot in front of the torso, knee slightly bent, and toes pointed forward. Set the right foot firmly on top of a step-up box or flat bench. Bend the right knee slightly, setting your body in a traditional lunge position. Set the torso upright with the eyes looking forward.

The Exercise: Set your core by contracting the abdominals, and descend the hips slowly towards the floor, bend both knees to do so. Continue to lower the hips towards the floor until the left thigh is parallel to the floor. Pause for one second and ascend slowly to the starting position of the exercise. Reset the bracing of the core and perform 8-15 repetitions of the exercise. Repeat with the opposite foot on the bench.

Tip: Maintain an upright torso throughout the exercise and brace the core for every repetition.

Good Mornings

Goal: Develop hinging movement of the hip and develop strength in the lower body.

Starting Position: Place the feet shoulder width apart, hands on the hips, and torso upright.

The Exercise: Begin the exercise by slowly pushing the hips backwards. Simultaneously lower the chest towards the floor by allowing the knees to bend slightly. Lower the chest as close to parallel to the floor as possible while keeping the back flat. Pause slightly, return to the starting position of the exercise and repeat for 8-15 repetitions.

Tip: Add a weight vest for additional resistance and focus on hinging at the hips.

Medicine Ball Dead Lift

Goal: Increase pull strength in the hips, lower back, and hamstrings.

Starting Position: Grasp a 3-6 lb. medicine ball with both hands. Place your feet shoulder width apart, body upright, and hands resting at hip level.

The Exercise: While maintaining a flat back, hinge at the hips, bend the knees slightly, and slowly lower the medicine ball downward the front of your thighs. Keep your eyes looking forward and bend the legs slightly. Continue to lower the medicine ball to shin level in a controlled manner. Return to the starting position of the exercise and repeat for 10-15 repetitions.

Tip: Keep your back flat, and push the hips backwards during the descending portion of the exercise.

Dumbbell Dead Lift

Goal: Develop bilateral pull strength in the lower body.

Starting Position: Grasp dumbbells, place the feet shoulder width apart, torso upright, and hands resting at thigh level.

The Exercise: Brace the core by contracting the abdominals. Hinge at the hip and begin to press the hips backwards as you slowly lower the dumbbells down the front of your thighs. Allow the knees to bend slightly and continue to lower the dumbbells downward to just below the knees. Pause slightly, return to the starting position of the exercise by extending at the knees and hips. Repeat the exercise sequence for 8-15 repetitions.

Tip: Pay strict attention technique, do not overload the exercise, and focus on pushing backwards with the hips.

Barbell Dead Lift

Goal: Increase pull strength in the lower body.

Starting Position: Grasp the barbell with both hands at shoulder width. Place the feet shoulder width apart, torso upright, and arms extended.

The Exercise: Brace the core by contracting the abdominals. Hinge at the hip and begin to press the hips backwards as you slowly lower the barbell down the front of your thighs. Allow the knees to bend slightly and continue to lower the barbell downward to just below the knees. Pause slightly, return to the starting position of the exercise by extending at the knees and hips. Repeat the exercise sequence for 8-15 repetitions.

Tip: Pay strict attention technique, do not overload the exercise, and focus on pushing backwards with the hips.

Single Leg Medicine Ball Dead Lift

Goal: Increase single leg pull strength in the hamstrings, hips, and lower back.

Starting Position: Grasp a 3-6 lb. medicine ball with both hands. Place the feet shoulder width apart, body upright, and hands in front of hips. Lift the right foot off the floor and balance on the left leg.

The Exercise: Brace the core by contracting the abdominals and slowly reach with the medicine ball down towards the left foot. Bend at your hips and keep the left leg straight. Continue to reach with the medicine ball towards the top of the foot. Allow the right leg to extend backwards as a counterbalance. Pause for one second at the bottom position of the exercise and return to the starting position. Exhale at the mid-point of your ascent. Perform 8-15 repetitions and repeat with the opposite leg.

Tip: Attempt to balance on one leg throughout the entire exercise.

Single Leg Suit Case Dumbbell Dead Lift

Goal: Increase unilateral lower body pull strength and improve balance.

Starting Position: Grasp a dumbbell or kettle bell with left hand. Place the feet shoulder width apart, body upright, and dumbbell resting on the side of the left hip. Lift the right foot off the floor and balance on the left leg.

The Exercise: Brace the core by contracting the abdominals and slowly reach down the side of the left leg to shin level with the dumbbell. Bend at your hips, keep the left leg straight, and allow the right leg to extend backwards as a counterbalance. Pause for one second at the bottom position of the exercise and return to the starting position. Exhale at the mid-point of your ascent. Perform 8-15 repetitions and repeat with the opposite leg.

Tip: Attempt to balance on one leg throughout the entire exercise.

Single Leg Dumbbell Dead Lift

Goal: Increase unilateral lower body pull strength and improve balance.

Starting Position: Grasp dumbbells with both hands. Place the feet shoulder width apart, body upright, and dumbbell resting in front of hips. Lift the right foot off the floor and balance on the left leg.

The Exercise: Brace the core by contracting the abdominals and slowly reach with the dumbbells down to shin level. Bend at your hips and keep the left leg straight. Continue to reach with the dumbbell towards the top of the foot. Allow the right leg to extend backwards as a counterbalance. Pause for one second at the bottom position of the exercise and return to the starting position. Exhale at the mid-point of your ascent. Perform 8-15 repetitions and repeat with the opposite leg.

Tip: Attempt to balance on one leg throughout the entire exercise.

Tubing Press

Goal: Develop upper body horizontal push strength.

Starting Position: Stand upright, knees slightly bent, and eyes looking forward. Grasp tubing with both hands next to the shoulders and elbows bent. Step 2-4 feet away from the tubing attachment to create some resistance.

The Exercise: Simultaneously press the hands forward, keeping the elbows elevated and torso upright. Continue to press forward until both arms are straight. Pause for one second and return to the starting position of the exercise. Repeat for 10-15 repetitions.

Tip: Keep your elbows elevated at shoulder height throughout the entire exercise.

Physio-Ball Push Up

Goal: Develop upper body push strength.

Starting Position: Place both hands on the side of the ball shoulder width apart, arms extended, leg straight, and feet together. Tighten the lower back, core, and place the hips inline with the shoulders and feet. An imaginary straight line should exist between the feet and shoulders in which the hips intersect. Do not allow the hips to elevate or sag during the entire exercise.

The Exercise: Slowly lower the chest towards the ball by bending the elbows. Continue to lower the chest until it touches the ball. Pause for one second, return to the starting position of the exercise and repeat for 8-15 repetitions. Maintain a rigid body position throughout and be sure to move through a full range of motion.

Tip: Add a weighted vest to increase the difficulty of the exercise.

Physio-Ball Dumbbell Chest Press

Goal: Increase upper body horizontal push strength.

Starting Position: Grasp dumbbells and lie with head and shoulders on the top of the ball. Place feet shoulder width apart on the floor and elevate hips to a position in line with your shoulders and knees. Place hands next to shoulders with palms facing your knees.

The Exercise: Extend your arms and press the dumbbells up. Continue to press upwards until the arms are straight. Return to the starting position and repeat for 8-15 repetitions.

Tip: Alternate the pressing of the arms to increase the difficulty of the exercise and always keep the hips elevated throughout the exercise.

Physio-Ball Single Arm Chest Press

Goal: Increase upper body horizontal unilateral push strength.

Starting Position: Grasp dumbbell with right hand and lie with head and shoulders on the top of the ball. Place feet shoulder width apart on the floor and elevate hips to a position in line with your shoulders and knees. Position right hand next to shoulder with palm facing your knees.

The Exercise: Extend your right arm and press the dumbbell up. Continue to press upwards until the arm is straight. Return to the starting position and repeat for 8-15 repetitions. Perform exercise with opposite arm.

Tip: Maintain bridge position of the body throughout the exercise.

Tall Kneeling Dumbbell Overhead Dumbbell Press

Goal: Increase vertical push strength.

Starting Position: Grasp a dumbbell in the left hand and position the lower body in a tall kneeling position with both knees on the floor. Position the torso in a tall upright position with the eyes looking forward. Place the dumbbell next to your left shoulder with the elbow pointing down towards the floor.

The Exercise: Extend your left arm and press the dumbbell up. Continue to press until the right arm is straight. Return to the starting position and repeat for 6-15 repetitions.

Tip: Keep your torso upright throughout the exercise and do not lock your elbow.

Kneeling Lunge Dumbbell Shoulder Press

Goal: Increase unilateral vertical push strength.

Starting Position: Grasp a dumbbell in the right hand and position the lower body in a kneeling lunge position with the right knee on the floor. Place feet shoulder width apart on the floor and eyes looking forward. Place the dumbbell next to your right shoulders with the elbow pointing down towards the floor.

The Exercise: Extend your right arm and press the dumbbell up. Continue to press until the right arm is straight. Return to the starting position and repeat for 6-15 repetitions.

Tip: Keep your torso upright throughout the exercise and do not lock your elbow.

Wide Grip Lat Pull Down

Goal: Develop upper body vertical pull strength.

Starting Position: Grasp the lat pulldown bar slightly wider than shoulder width. Sit with knees bent, feet firmly on the floor, arms extended, and torso upright.

The Exercise: Pull the shoulders downward and shoulder blades together. Once the shoulders are "set in position" begin pulling bar downward towards the top of your chest by bending the arms. Continue to pull downward until the bar touches your chest at the collarbone. Pause briefly, return to the starting position, and repeat for 8-15 repetitions.

Tip: Maintain an upright torso throughout the exercise and use your back muscles to perform the exercise.

Single Arm Lat Pull Down

Goal: Develop unilateral strength in the upper back and shoulders.

Starting Position: Grasp a single handle cable attachment with the right hand. Sit with knees bent, feet firmly on the floor, arms extended, and torso upright.

The Exercise: Set the right shoulder by pulling downward with the shoulder blade. Once the right shoulder is in a "set in position" begin pulling the right hand downward towards the top of your chest by bending the arm. Continue to pull downward until the handle touches your chest at the collarbone. Pause briefly, return to the starting position, and repeat for 8-15 repetitions. Repeat the exercise sequence with the left arm.

Tip: Maintain an upright torso, do not rotate right or left throughout the exercise, and use your back muscles to perform the exercise.

Pull Up

Goal: Develop upper body pull strength in the posterior chain.

Starting Position: grasp a pull up bar slightly wider than shoulder width with palms facing away from you. Extend the arms straight allowing the body to hang directly below the fixed bar.

The Exercise: Begin pulling upwards by bending both elbows. Continue to pull upwards until your chin is above the bar. Pause for one second, return to the starting position, and perform 8-15 repetitions.

Tip: Use the assistance of a spotter if needed to complete the suggested number of repetitions. Increase the difficulty of this exercise with a weighted vest.

Tubing Row

Goal: Increase horizontal pull strength.

Starting Position: Stand upright, knees slightly bent, and eyes looking forward. Grasp tubing with both hands at shoulder height with both arms straight. Step 2-4 feet away from the tubing attachment to create resistance.

The Exercise: Begin the exercise by pulling both arms backwards by bending the elbows. Continue to pull backwards until the hands are next to both shoulders. Pause for one second and return to the starting position of the exercise. Repeat for 6-15 repetitions.

Tip: Maintain and upright torso throughout the entire exercise.

Horizontal Pull Up

Goal: Increase horizontal upper body pull strength.

Starting Position: Place an Olympic bar on a squat rack at a height where you are able to hang underneath it. Lie flat on your back with the bar directly above the chest, legs straight, feet together, and torso rigid. Grasp the bar with both hands shoulder width apart pulling the body slightly off the floor.

The Exercise: Pull the upper body towards the bar keeping the feet in place and the legs straight. Continue to pull upward until your chest is touching the bar. Pause slightly, return to the starting position of the exercise and repeat. Keep the torso and legs straight throughout the exercise. Perform 8-15 repetitions of the exercise.

Tip: Increase the difficulty of the exercise by setting the feet on top of a bench or physio-ball. Always keep the body straight throughout the entire exercise.

Single Arm Dumbbell Row

Goal: Develop unilateral upper body horizontal pull strength.

Starting position: Grasp a dumbbell with the right hand and place the left hand with the arm slightly bent on top of a bench. Set the feet shoulder width apart, knees bent, hips pressed backwards, and back flat. Extend the right arm straight while maintaining position of your body.

The Exercise: Pull the dumbbell upward towards your torso by bending the right elbow. Continue to pull upward until your hand is next to the rib cage. Pause slightly, return to the starting position of the exercise and repeat for 8-15 repetitions. Repeat the exercise sequence with the opposition hand.

Tip: Maintain position of the torso, hips, and legs throughout the entire exercise.

Summary

This chapter has provided the principles to follow in the set-up of the functional training section of your program. Remember a golf specific conditioning program requires it to be: multi-dimensional, multi-planar, cross specific, progressive, systematic, and force output orientated. Ignoring one of these principles negates a portion of accomplishments from your program, and will hinder your success. Keep in mind functional strength training for golf requires you to develop lower body push, lower body pull, upper body push, and upper body pull strength. As a result it is imperative to utilize exercise developing all of the aforementioned strength planes. Listed below are some sample functional strength programs to provide you an idea of how to develop this section of your program.

Table 1.9 Sample Functional Strength Programs

BEGINNER PROGRAM

Monday:	Lower Body Push - BW Squat	2 sets x 10 repetitions
	Upper Body Pull - Tubing Row	2 sets x 10 repetitions
	Lower Body Pull - Good Morning	2 sets x 10 repetitions
	Upper Body Push - Tubing Press	2 sets x 10 repetitions
Wednesday:	Lower Body Push - BW Squat	2 sets x 10 repetitions
	Upper Body Pull - Tubing Row	2 sets x 10 repetitions
	Lower Body Pull - Good Morning	2 sets x 10 repetitions
	Upper Body Push - Tubing Press	2 sets x 10 repetitions
Friday:	Lower Body Push - BW Squat	2 sets x 10 repetitions
	Upper Body Pull - Tubing Row	2 sets x 10 repetitions
	Lower Body Pull - Good Morning	2 sets x 10 repetitions
	Upper Body Push - Tubing Press	2 sets x 10 repetitions

INTERMEDIATE PROGRAM

Monday:	Lower Body Push - Jefferson Squat	2 sets x 10 repetitions
	Upper Body Pull - Wide Grip Lat Pull Down	2 sets x 10 repetitions
	Lower Body Pull - Medicine Ball Dead Lift	2 set x 10 repetitions

	Upper Body Push - Physio- Ball Push Up	2 sets x 10 repetitions
Wednesday:	Lower Body Push - Bulgarian Spilt Squat	2 sets x 10 repetitions
	Upper Body Pull - Horizontal Row	2 sets x 10 repetitions
	Lower Body Pull - Med Ball Single Leg Dead Lift	2 sets x 10 repetitions
	Upper Body Push - Tall Kneeling DB OH Press	2 sets x 10 repetitions
Friday:	Lower Body Push - Jefferson Squat	2 sets x 10 repetitions
	Upper Body Pull - Wide Grip Lat Pull Down	2 sets x 10 repetitions
	Lower Body Pull - Medicine Ball Dead Lift	2 sets x 10 repetitions
	Upper Body Push - Physio-Ball Push Up	2 sets x 10 repetitions

ADVANCED PROGRAM

Monday:	Lower Body Push - Dumbbell Goblet Squat	3 sets x 8 repetitions
	Upper Body Pull - Wide Grip Pull Up	3 sets x 8 repetitions
Tuesday:	Lower Body Pull - Dumbbell Dead Lift	3 sets x 8 repetitions
	Upper Body Push - Physio-Ball DB Chest Press	3 sets x 8 repetitions
Thursday:	Lower Body Push - Bulgarian Split Squat w/ DB	3 sets x 8 repetitions
	Upper Body Pull - Single Arm Dumbbell Row	3 sets x 8 repetitions
Friday:	Lower Body Pull - Single Leg Dumbbell Dead Lift	3 sets x 8 repetitions
	Upper Body Push - Kneeling Lunge DB Press	3 sets x 8 repetitions

Chapter Eleven
Anaerobic Training, Aerobics, Nutrition, and Recovery

The previous chapters of this book have discussed the physical parameters required in the development of the pitcher. Areas to discuss in this chapter are the areas of anaerobic training, aerobic conditioning, nutrition, and recovery. It is interesting when we present these topics the thought which "pops" into most golfers minds is aerobic training equals fat loss.

You go back a decade or two and talk to someone in the health and fitness industry, aerobic training was a key component to fat loss, higher fitness levels, and better. This concept has changed drastically but unfortunately for the majority of the population, the concept of aerobic training and benefits of this modality have not changed in 30 years. Yes, aerobic training can assist in fat loss, fitness levels, and body composition, but it is not as valuable a commodity as we once perceived.

Fast forward to this decade and the strength and conditioning coach will utilize aerobic conditioning though admittedly much less . The process incorporates much more anaerobic or interval based philosophy. In this day and age I believe we have a found a good balance and understand the purpose of both aerobic and anaerobic conditioning for the golfer.

Aerobic Conditioning

Aerobic conditioning can benefit any individual from junior player to professional. Aerobic conditioning improves the cardio-pulmonary outputs of the body for health and wellness. Aerobic conditioning has its' place in a comprehensive strength and conditioning program.

The goal of aerobic conditioning is not to increase your oxygen uptake or VO2 max: anaerobic conditioning does that. Aerobic conditioning is very inefficient in terms of fat loss and changes in body composition. Aerobic conditioning moves oxygen through the body allowing for an increase in the transportation of oxygen and nutrients to working muscles. Such activity assists in tissue repair and the recovery process of the body. Aerobic conditioning can provide a benefit in terms of promoting oxygen and blood flow for tissue repair.

The type, frequency and amount of aerobic exercise one should incorporate into their training is very much dependent training variables and time available in your schedule. The duration and frequency of aerobic training can range from 2-4 days per week and session times of 20-45 minutes.

Numerous choices such as running at a moderate pace, stationary biking, or even the treadmill in the weight room exist for your aerobic conditioning. The modality chosen to complete this section of your training is again determined by individual factors. Regardless of the choice in aerobic training modalities, it is very important to execute your aerobic conditioning at the correct intensity. A simple test I utilize to determine if you are working at a good intensity is the "talk test". During your aerobic training session, train at a level where you are working hard, but still able to have a normal conversation with someone standing next to you. Relative to your golf fitness training, it is ideal to place aerobic training sessions at the end of your program.

Anaerobic Conditioning

The modalities, execution of exercises, outcome and variables associated with anaerobic training are completely different than those of aerobic conditioning. The goal of anaerobic training is to improve the oxygen uptake capacities of your cardiovascular system (measured uniformly by your VO2 max). Let's take an example of anaerobic activity to better define and understand it. By products of anaerobic conditioning are improved levels of stamina (important on the back nine and when playing back to back days), changes in body composition, and fat loss. Research in recent years indicates interval training is by far a much more efficient means to loose body fat and change body composition.

Sprint work may be the easiest example of anaerobic training to understand. Sprinting a specified distance for a certain number of repetitions with a rest interval in between each sprint will increase over time the efficiency at which oxygen uptake occurs, thus improving your VO2 max and anaerobic capacities. Interval springs is a prime example of a common anaerobic conditioning activity where you sprint for 20 yards, walk 20 yards, and sprint again.

The benefits of anaerobic training are; an increase in the amount and rate of oxygen that is delivered to working muscles, a decrease in the rate at which muscular fatigue sets in during physical activity, a reduced recovery time and increases in speed. All of which are beneficial to the pitcher. That being said anaerobic conditioning is a very necessary part of the competitive golfer's conditioning program.

Relative to the golfers there are a number of choices in terms of anaerobic training modalities. This again depends upon the time available and what is available in terms of equipment and facilities. Jump rope intervals are a great anaerobic training modality. A heavy or light rope can be used for this exercise and slight changes in effort levels should be made during the season relative to the off-season. Another beneficial anaerobic training modality for golfers is interval sprints on the bike. Simply use a stationary bike and create an interval time of maximum effort followed by a rest period. Regardless of the modality chosen to complete your anaerobic training, a time frame of 8-10 minutes should suffice for this section of your training. The frequency of anaerobic training is dictated by time available in your schedule. Anaerobic training should be performed at least 1-2 times per week. 3 times per week would be ideal.

Nutrition

The food consumed on a daily basis and during a round of golf will affect how well you play. I utilize the phrase "food is fuel" when discussing nutrition relative to the athlete. Good nutrition equals good fuel for the body and results in you feeling better and playing better. On the flip side, poor nutrition equals bad fuel causing less than optimal play and poor health.

All too often nutrition is forgotten in the minds of the golfer and overlooked as it relates to health, wellness, improved physical conditioning, and recovery. That being said, golfers of any age can improve their health, wellness and game with sound nutrition.

Nutrition can be very basic. Essentially what will affect your round. It is key when on the course to provide your body with proper hydration and fuel during the course of the game. It is best to hydrate with water or a sports drink during a game. A fuel source in the form of complex carbohydrates, good fats, and proteins will provide sustained energy from the first pitch to the last. Convenient food sources such as nuts, fruits, and certain nutritional bars are ideal for your round of golf.

To achieve a sensible diet grounded upon basic nutrition is quite easy. In the most basic of terms we have carbohydrates, fats, and proteins. I break each of these categories down into "good" and "bad". Eat good carbohydrates, fats and proteins you will do splendidly. Consume too many "bad" carbohydrates, fats and proteins problems will occur. Now let's take a look at each of these categories to allow you a better understanding on how what you eat impacts your performance.

Carbohydrates are the main fuel source for the body. Carbohydrates are broken down into sugar by your body and used for energy. Energy to walk, talk, drive a car, and swing a club. We need carbohydrates to function on a day-to-day basis. The key component as it relates to carbohydrates is the type ("good" or "bad"). Good carbohydrates consist of complex sugars that are burned slowly by the body, providing you long-term energy. Bad carbohydrates consist of simple sugars, which are burned very quickly, causing spikes in blood sugar, and bouts of low energy. Sources of good carbohydrates are apples, whole grain breads, beans, all-bran cereals, and whole oats. Bad carbohydrates are any foods containing large amounts of simple sugars such as candy bars, donuts, soda, and white bread. Basically, avoid foods with bad carbohydrates and eat the good ones.

Proteins are commonly referred to as "the building blocks of the body". The reason for this is proteins assist in the repair and building of new tissue. Any activity involving your muscles causes the breakdown of tissue within the body. In order to repair this tissue and build new tissue the body requires sources of protein. For example, golf fitness exercises require exertion from your muscles. This activity creates micro-tears in your muscles. In order to repair these micro-tears, protein is required.

Good proteins can be classified as lean cuts of beef, chicken, turkey, fish, eggs, tofu, and even nuts. Bad proteins contain a high level of saturated fats either naturally or from having been cooked in bad fats. For example, a lean cut of beef cooked in butter becomes a bad protein; not because of the protein source itself, but rather from it being cooked in butter. Stick with lean cuts of beef, skinless chicken, turkey, fish, and nuts for your protein sources. Avoid foods that are fried, and pay attention to how you cook it. Do note the body can use protein as an energy source but it is much better off with energy supplied from good fats and carbohydrates.

All too often fats are thought of as bad for your health. This is a misconception. Your body requires the consumption of some fats for day-to-day functioning. Just as carbohydrates and proteins can either be good or bad, fats can as well. Good fats can be found in food sources such as avocados, salmon, nuts, and olive oil. These fats sources provide your body with long-term energy sources as well as assisting in the transfer of nutrients at a cellular level. Bad fats, on the other hand, contain high levels of saturated fat and are not used efficiently by the body. Butter, bacon, fatty meats, fried chicken, French fries, potato chips, and many fast food items should be avoided. Basically, avoid bad fats and consume sources of good fats.

Results in your strength and conditioning program require sound nutrition. The body must be provided with good sources of fuel on and off the mound. This will allow for the gains you are attempting to make as a golfer become a reality.

Improvement of your nutrition is a long-term project; there are no "quick fixes" as it pertains to healthy nutrition. I suggest thinking about nutrition as you do improving as a pitcher; it takes time, dedication, and commitment to the right food choices. Put a plan in place, be dedicated to that plan, and be patient. Dividends in your game will be the result.

Recovery

Aerobic conditioning, anaerobic conditioning, and nutrition have been the focal points of this chapter. A fourth component, recovery, requires attention as well. Recovery can be defined as the process of your body repairing and preparing itself for daily life, physical activity, training, and/or sport. Repairing is defined as the process of providing your body the proper rest/nutrition, preparing is the physical task of training/practice to perform your chosen sport. Recovery incorporates both the preparation and repairing process.

Recovery for golfers is broken down into two segments. Segment number one is the recovery time between sets and exercises within your training program. Recovery time (i.e. rest periods) between sets/exercises drastically affects the physical outcome of your golf fitness training. For example, if you were in the power training section of your training program and resting only 30 seconds between each set of overhead medicine ball throws, this would be too little of a rest between each set of exercises for this type of training. The incorrect rest period in the above example would result in less gain from the exercise.

The table below breaks down the ideal rest periods between each segment of your training program. Table 1.7 will assist in determining the proper rest periods between each set of exercise in your strength and conditioning program.

Table 1.10 Recovery Time for Exercise Modalities

TYPE OF TRAINING	REPETITION/SETS	REST PERIODS	FREQUENCY WORKOUTS
Warm-up	5-15	Minimal	6
Flexibility	30-45 sec. Hold	Minimal	4-6
Balance	8-15	30 seconds	3-4
Core Strength	6-15	30 seconds	3-4
Functional Strength	5-12	60 seconds	3-4
Power	3-10	2 minutes	2-3

The above table clearly indicates how recovery time significantly affects the outcome of your training program. Utilize this table in accordance to the segment of your program to obtain the greatest benefit from your training.

The second segment of recovery encompasses the rest period between your workouts. Table 1.7, in addition to providing information on rest periods between sets, also offers information on the frequency of your training. For example, warm-up and flexibility training require little recovery time for your body. This allows you to implement these segments more frequently into your program, almost on a daily basis. Balance, torso strength, and functional strength exercises necessitate a larger recovery period between exercise bouts. A recovery time of anywhere between 24-36 hours is needed for these types of exercises. Power is on the other side of the spectrum relative to warm-up/flexibility exercises. This type of training requires 48-72 hours between sessions. These recovery periods allow your body to repair micro-trauma resulting from the workout. In addition, following these recovery guidelines between exercise sessions will prepare your body for the next training session.

It is very important to keep in mind recovery is an essential component of any training program. Too much training can result in less than optimal results from your program, and, in addition, can be counterproductive to your throwing program.

Summary

Advancement in your game not only requires improving as a golfer and fitness components of the body, but also requires the inclusion of aerobic training, anaerobic training, sound nutrition, and proper recovery. The incorporation of these components into your comprehensive game improvement program will provide you with the greatest amount of success from your efforts on and off the mound.

Chapter Twelve

Strength & Conditioning Programs

We are now ready to put all this information into your own training program. Chapter 12 will present you with guidelines to design, implement, and alter your workout program to your own individual needs and schedule. While reading through this chapter keep in mind all the information you have previous learned. Refer back to previous chapters if necessary. This is the point where you design a training program to your specific needs and goals as a golfer.

Before beginning your golf specific training program, you must determine that goals and needs of your training. For example, if you find that you are lacking the needed core strength to stabilize the body and rotate around a fixed spine angle. Then a specific portion should focus on the development of additional core and joint integrity strength/endurance. This chapter will begin by guiding you through the process of designing of your own training program. Golfer specific training programs for beginners to advanced players will be reviewed, and an introduction of some advanced training techniques will be presented for your viewing. Individuals with a strong background in resistance training may utilize the more advanced training techniques immediately. Always remember to be cross specific with all of your training modalities.

Program Design

Every individual will have different goals, exercises, and variables within their golf specific training program. Due to this reason, the first step in any resistance training program is determining your personal needs. The second step is to develop a training program that meets those needs. These two parameters require you to start off with what is termed a "needs analysis". The second step within this process after an assessment is determining what your goals are within this training program. You must initially invest a little time on these two steps or you will find yourself putting in a great deal of time and effort into a training program, and getting marginal results!

Needs Analysis and Training Goals

A needs analysis essentially entails determining what requirements your golf specific training must meet. Two areas must be focused upon when preparing your needs analysis. Discussed many times throughout this book has been the idea of cross specificity: train specifically to the positions, movements, and athletic requirements of a golfer. At this point you want to further delineate this concept to what you need as a golfer. For example, a professional golfer on the PGA Tour has definitively different requirements of their training program than does the recreational level player looking to lower their handicap and get rid of that nagging lower back pain.

This will allow for a more specialized program to be developed. The second factor of information that needs to be attained from your "needs analysis" is individual areas that need improvement. For example, if you are lacking strength endurance in the lower extremities (i.e. legs/hips), then a key to a portion of your training needs to focus on developing this parameter in the legs and torso. Overall, your analysis process aims at developing a map of specific neuromuscular requirements that are needed by you as a golfer. The analysis will also highlight the areas that require your attention to improve as an individual ball player.

The final step is mapping out your training goals. Once you have determined the "needs" of your position on the staff, and your "needs" as an individual, a list of training goals for your training program may be developed. The main goal of your training is to improve yourself as a golfer, but as stated above there may areas that need additional attention. Listed below are the goals of a comprehensive golf specific training program.

Golf Specific Training Program Goals

- *Develop required joint mobility*
- *Improve balance*
- *Improved stabilization*
- *Increase in core strength/endurance/power*
- *Improvement in neuromuscular flexibility parameters*
- *Neuromuscular endurance*
- *Development of neuromuscular strength endurance*
- *Increased neuromuscular strength*
- *Improved neuromuscular power outputs*
- *Increases in neuromuscular endurance*
- *Improve lower back health*
- *Improve stamina*

You can see from the above list that a golf specific training program has many areas that it directs you in terms of developing your neuromuscular system. This brings us to the point of putting all the information in this book into a sequential order to follow during your day-to-day training.

Order of Golf Specific Training Program

An ideal golf specific training program follows a sequence. The recommended sequence to follow on a day-to-day basis, this allows for proper ratios of balance, stabilization, flexibility, core, joint stabilization, resistance training exercises, power, aerobic and anaerobic exercises to be performed.

Warm up, Flexibility, and Mobility Exercises

The dynamic warm up, flexibility, mobility, and corrective exercises is the first section of your programming and always should be. The foam roll, static flexibility, dynamic range of motion, and mobility exercises not only develop the required levels of flexibility and mobility in the kinetic chain but also prepare the body. This preparation is via activation and moving the body through multi-joing/multi-directional movement patterns.

Power Exercises

The next series of protocols in your individualized golf training program are power drills. Make sure before you begin any power training activities you have developed a foundation within your neuromuscular system. This foundation is a direct result of your balance, stabilization, core, and functional training. Allow at least 4 to 6 weeks of consisted training with the modalities listed above to allow for a base of "strength" in these parameters to have been developed. The goals of your power exercises are to develop speed and power within the neuromuscular system. At times with younger players this section of the program may be moved behind the core section of the training program. The reason behind such a shift is prioritization of training goals within the individual player.

Balance and Core Exercises

A very important segment of your training are the capacities of balance, stabilization, and core strength/endurance. If your balance capacities, segmental stabilization, and core are not developed to a high level and are less than optimal, the ability to execute an efficient swing, generate power, and reduce the potential for injury will be minimal. A "weak core" places greater stresses on the lower back and we can obviously see the concerns with such a situation.

These exercises focus on developing the parameters of balance and stabilization in the entire neuromuscular system. The core strengthening exercises will develop strength, strength endurance, and power in the core section of the body. If the torso section of the body is ignored then again the strength/power created in the extremities will be less than optimal because energy transferred through the kinetic chain will be limited by the weak musculature area of the torso.

Functional Exercise

At this point you are ready to start your functional strength training exercises. Remember, these exercises are cross specific to the positions, movements, and neuromuscular actions that you perform in this sport. The rational behind cross specificity training is the transfer of training effect. Training the neuromuscular system specific to the positions, movements, and actions results in a optimal performance on the course. If your resistance training exercises are not cross specific then the results from your hard work will be less than optimal. As a result of the requirements of a golfer, your functional resistance training protocols will incorporate multi-planar, multi-dimensional, endurance, strength endurance, power, speed, and balance exercises.

Up to this point we have reviewed the proper training sequence for a golf specific conditioning program. The sequence is as follows: (1) dynamic warm up, flexibility, and mobility exercises, (2) power training, (3) balance/stabilization/core exercises, and (4) functional resistance training exercises. This gives you an outline to follow when developing your individualized golf specific conditioning/training program. At this point, a series of sample conditioning programs will be presented for beginners to advance.

Periodization Schedules

Recalling chapter two, periodization is a process of cycling loads, volumes, intensity, and exercises within a given time period. The times frames can be divided into weeks, months and even years. Each time frame has a specific arrangement of load, volume, intensity, and exercises within the given time frame. The cycles of a periodization program are broken down into macrocycles and microcycles.

A macrocycle is the complete training time, which is usually one year. A mesocycle is a specific time frame within the macrocycle (for example, one baseball season). The mesocycle is usually planned around the differing portions of the year for the ball player (in-season, off-season, pre-season). The subdivisions of mesocycles for golf in a linear periodization schedule are as follows:

Phase 1: strength and endurance training. The body gains muscular strength and endurance.

Phase 2: strength training. The body continues strength development in the muscular system and power training is introduced. Training intensity increases and overall volume remains the same or decreases.

Phase 3: power training: The body develops increased power outputs. Training intensity increases and overall volume decreases.

Phase 4: sports-specific training: Sport-specific movements are refined, and the athlete focuses upon the upcoming season. Training intensity and volume decreases.

Phase 5: competition/maintenance training. Intensity is lower and volume decreased so that the athlete can on competition.

The professional golfer will typically find phases 1, 2, and 3 in the off-season portion of their program, phase 4 in the pre-season, and phase 5 during the season. The phases within the periodization program allow for a systematic introduction of increased training intensities, volumes, and additional variables into the golfer's training program. This allows the body to gradually adapt to new stresses placed upon it and peak correctly for key events during the season.

Utilizing a scheme popularized by strength and conditioning coach Janet Alexander, we can input the mesocycle phases listed above into "blocks" for the off-season, pre-season, and in-season phases of the mesocycle. Each block represents one 7-day training week. For example, block number one in the off-season represents the first week of training during the off-season training schedule. Block number two represents the second week of the off-season schedule and each consecutive block would correlate to the next week for the remainder of the off-season schedule. Using this system of blocks creates a very simple process in terms of developing a golfer's off-season, pre-season and in-season periodization schedule. All that is required for the utilization of the block system is to determine the number of weeks each segment (off-season, pre-season, in-season) will contain within the year for the golfer.

For example, a professional golfer typically has an 6-10 week off-season training time after an active rest post-season, this portion of the periodization schedule would then contain six to ten blocks (one block for each week). Each block representing one week would have a specific training goal with corresponding training volumes, intensities and exercises to achieve this goal. The tendency for most athletes in the off-season would have blocks 1-4 work on developing phase 1 of the mesocycle, blocks 5-8 build phase 2 of the mesocycle, and blocks 9-12 train phase 3 of the mesocycle.

I am a strong proponent of both periodization schedules and Janet Alexander's block system in the implementation of training for athletes. Such programs allow for a systematic, structured and measurable process to occur in the training of these young athletes. I personally utilize both perdiozation schedules and the block system and would recommend you do the same.

Beginner Strength & Conditioning Program

Up to this point in this chapter we have discussed the importance of a needs analysis, goal setting and periodization schedules. We will now begin to assimilate all this information into a series of sample strength and conditioning programs. It is important to note the programs listed below are simply sample programs and are to be used only as guidelines in the development of your own individualized training program. The first sample program listed is the beginner strength and conditioning program.

The beginner program is ideal for the individual new to resistance training. I personally find it best to start all junior level players with a beginner lever program for the shear fact many of the exercises and training modalities are new for the athlete regardless of training experience. After the commencement of a beginner level program plan to spend 8 to 12 weeks at this level before moving onto the next. A time frame of 8 to 12 weeks will allow for your body to adapt to the new exercises, provide time for improvement in key areas for golf, and mastery of this program.

For the benefits of this program to become a reality it is imperative that you are consistent with your training. If you are consistent with your training, physical benefits and improvement should begin to be seen within 4-6 weeks.

It is strongly suggested you follow the program sequence listed in the first section of this chapter. Begin with a foam rolling, move onto your flexibility exercises, proceed to your balance training and complete the program with the core strength and functional exercises. This will provide your body the proper ratios of each type of training for improvement in your golf game. Power training is not a component of the beginner program because this type of training requires a base of flexibility, balance, strength, and endurance to perform correctly. This program will develop the foundation required for power training.

Guidelines:

3 times per week   1 set per exercise   5-15 repetitions per set

Foam Roll Exercises:	Sets:	Repetitions:
Calf Foam Roll	1	5
Glute Foam Roll	1	5
IT Band Foam Roll	1	5
Quadriceps Foam Roll	1	5
Thoracic Foam Roll	1	5
Lat Foam Roll	1	5

Flexibility Exercises:	Sets:	Repetitions
90/90 Hamstring Stretch	1	30 second hold
Piriformis Stretch	1	30 second hold
Glute Stretch	1	30 second hold
Kneeling Hip Flexor	1	30 second hold

Side Lunge Stretch	1	30 second hold
Lat Stretch w/ Physio–Ball	1	30 second hold
Chest Stretch w/ Physio-Ball	1	30 second hold

Functional Warm-up Exercises:	**Sets:**	**Repetitions**
Bent Knee Press Up	1	10
Flat Bench Hip Extension	1	10
Alternating Arm & Leg Extension	1	10
Thoracic Spine Openers	1	10
Plank Scapular Push Up	1	10
Tubing Walks	1	10
Stork Turns	1	10

Balance Exercises:	**Sets:**	**Repetitions:**
Single Leg Address Position	1	30 seconds

Core Strength Exercises:	**Sets:**	**Repetitions:**
Bent Knee Back Hold	1	30 second hold
Prone Hold	1	30 second hold
Side Hold	1	30 second hold

Scapular Integrity Exercises:	**Sets:**	**Repetitions:**
Exercise Ball Y-T-W-L	1	10

Functional Exercises:	**Sets:**	**Repetitions:**
Body Weight Squats	1	10
Tubing Row	1	10
Good Mornings	1	10
Tubing Press	1	10

Intermediate Strength & Conditioning Program

The intermediate program is the next program as you advance. It will introduce power training into the program. At this time the athlete should be ready for the implementation of such exercises. Advancement from the beginner level to the intermediate level will occur within 8-12 weeks assuming you were consistent with your training.

The exercises found in the intermediate program will be more challenging, and the program will continue the progress seen in your swing from the beginner level program. In addition to the exercises becoming more challenging, the option to increase the frequency of your training from 3 days per week to 4 exists.

Always keep in mind with the intermediate program, in addition to the other sample programs found in this book, the uniqueness of every athlete. Each and every athlete has different needs and goals as it relates to training. As a result there is no one program that is the correct training program for every individual golfer. The sample programs found in this book must be individualized to one's own requirements. Keep this point in mind and individualize each program to suit your own needs and goals.

Listed below are two sample intermediate level programs. Refer back to previous chapters for specific descriptions of each exercise. Execute each exercise with correct technique for the number of repetitions suggested. Do not compromise the form of each exercise to achieve a specific number of repetitions: rather perform the number of repetitions for the given exercise you can complete correctly.

Intermediate Strength & Conditioning Program One

Guidelines:

3 times per week   1-3 sets per exercise   5-15 repetitions per set

Foam Roll Exercises:	Sets:	Repetitions:
Calf Foam Roll	1	5
Glute Foam Roll	1	5
IT Band Foam Roll	1	5
Quadriceps Foam Roll	1	5
Thoracic Foam Roll	1	5
Lat Foam Roll	1	5

Flexibility Exercises:	Sets:	Repetitions:
90/90 Hamstring Stretch	1	30 second hold
Piriformis Stretch	1	30 second hold
Glute Stretch	1	30 second hold
Kneeling Hip Flexor	1	30 second hold
Cat In-the –Wheel	1	30 second hold
Side Lunge Stretch	1	30 second hold
Lat Stretch w/ Physio– Ball	1	30 second hold
Physio-Ball Chest Stretch	1	30 seconds hold

Functional Warm-up Exercises:	Sets:	Repetitions:
Bent Knee Press Up	1	10
Flat Bench Hip Extension	1	10
Alternating Arm & Leg Extension	1	10
Thoracic Spine Openers	1	10

Plank Scapular Push Up	1	10
Tubing Walks	1	10
Forward Lunge w/ Reach	1	10
Side Lunge w/ Reach	1	10
Spider	1	10

Power Exercises:	**Sets:**	**Repetitions:**
Kneeling Medicine Ball Side Throw	2	10
Box Jump	2	10
Medicine Ball Overhead Throw	2	10

Balance Exercises:	**Sets:**	**Repetitions:**
Single Leg Cone Reach	1	10
Single Leg Toe Touch	1	10

Core Strength Exercises:	**Sets:**	**Repetitions:**
Physio-Ball Saws	1	15
Physio-Ball Bent Knee Press Up	1	15
Cable Press Out	1	15

Scapular Integrity Exercises:	**Sets:**	**Repetitions:**
Exercise Ball Y-T-W-L	1	12

Functional Exercises:	**Sets:**	**Repetitions:**
Jefferson Squat	2	8
Suite Case Dead Lift	2	8
Physio-Ball Chest Press	2	8
Wide Grip Lat Pull Down	2	8
Single Arm Dumbbell Row	2	8

Anaerobic Conditioning:

40-yard Sprint Intervals (40 yard sprint, 30 seconds rest) x 4

Intermediate Strength & Conditioning Program Two

Guidelines:

4 times per week   Alternate between Program A and B   1-3 sets per exercise   5-20 repetitions per set

Program A

Foam Roll Exercises:	Sets:	Repetitions:
Calf Foam Roll	1	5
Glute Foam Roll	1	5
IT Band Foam Roll	1	5
Adductors Foam Roll	1	5
Thoracic Foam Roll	1	5
Lat Foam Roll	1	5

Flexibility Exercises:	Sets:	Repetitions
90/90 Hamstring Stretch	1	30 second hold
Piriformis Stretch	1	30 second hold
Glute Stretch	1	30 second hold
Kneeling Hip Flexor	1	30 second hold
Side Lunge Stretch	1	30 second hold
Lat Stretch w/ Physio– Ball	1	30 second hold
Physio-Ball Chest Stretch	1	30 seconds hold

Functional Warm-up Exercises:	Sets:	Repetitions
Bent Knee Press Up	1	10
Flat Bench Hip Extension	1	10
Alternating Arm & Leg Extension	1	10
Thoracic Spine Openers	1	10
Plank Scapular Push Up	1	10
Tubing Walks	1	10
Sumo Squat	1	10
Forward Lunge w/ Reach	1	10
Inch Worm	1	10

Balance Exercises:	Sets:	Repetitions:
Single Leg Airplane Rotations	1	10

Power Exercises:	Sets:	Repetitions:
Kneeling Medicine Ball Side Throw	2	10
Medicine Ball Overhead Throw	2	8

Core Strength Exercises:	Sets:	Repetitions:
Physio-Ball Saws	2	15
Physio-Ball Bent Knee Back Press	2	15

Functional Exercises:	Sets:	Repetitions:
Jefferson Squat	2	8
Physio-Ball DB Chest Press	2	8
Bulgarian Split Squat w/ Weight Vest	2	8
Tall Kneeling DB Press	2	8

Anaerobic Conditioning:

40-yard Sprint Intervals (40 yard sprint, 30 seconds rest) x 5

Program B

Foam Roll Exercises:	Sets:	Repetitions:
Calf Foam Roll	1	5
Glute Foam Roll	1	5
IT Band Foam Roll	1	5
Adductors Foam Roll	1	5
Thoracic Foam Roll	1	5
Lat Foam Roll	1	5

Flexibility Exercises:	Sets:	Repetitions
90/90 Hamstring Stretch	1	30 second hold
Piriformis Stretch	1	30 second hold
Glute Stretch	1	30 second hold
Kneeling Hip Flexor	1	30 second hold
Side Lunge Stretch	1	30 second hold
Lat Stretch w/ Physio– Ball	1	30 second hold
Physio-Ball Chest Stretch	1	30 seconds hold

Functional Warm-up Exercises:	Sets:	Repetitions
Bent Knee Press Up	1	10
Flat Bench Hip Extension	1	10

	Sets	Repetitions
Alternating Arm & Leg Extension	1	10
Thoracic Spine Openers	1	10
Plank Scapular Push Up	1	10
Tubing Walks	1	10
Sumo Squat	1	10
Side Lung w/ Reach	1	10
Spider	1	10

Power Exercises:	Sets:	Repetitions:
Medicine Ball Power Drops	2	10
Box Jump	2	10

Balance Exercises:	Sets:	Repetitions:
Single Leg Cone Reach	1	10
Single Leg Toe Touch	1	10

Core Strength Exercises:	Sets:	Repetitions:
Physio-Ball Table Top	2	15
Cable Press Outs	2	15

Scapular Integrity Exercises:	Sets:	Repetitions:
Kneeling Y-T-W-L	1	12

Functional Exercises:	Sets:	Repetitions:
Dumbbell Dead Lift	2	8
Single Arm Lat Pull Down	2	8
Single Leg Suit Case Dead Lift	2	8
Horizontal Bar Row	2	8

Advanced Strength & Conditioning Program

Once you have trained at the intermediate level program for 8 to 12 weeks, it is time to move onto the advanced level program. The intensity level will again increase at this level. Two advanced level training programs are delineated below. Again, it is recommended to adjust the sample programs to meet your own individual needs. Refer back to previous chapters for detailed exercise descriptions, pay strict attention to technique and perform the exercises to the best of your ability.

Advanced Strength & Conditioning Program One

Guidelines:

3 times per week	1-3 sets per exercise	5-15 repetitions per set

Foam Roll Exercises:	Sets:	Repetitions:
Calf Foam Roll	1	5
Glute Foam Roll	1	5
IT Band Foam Roll	1	5
Adductors Foam Roll	1	5
Thoracic Foam Roll	1	5
Lat Foam Roll	1	5

Flexibility Exercises:	Sets:	Repetitions
90/90 Hamstring Stretch	1	30 second hold
Piriformis Stretch	1	30 second hold
Glute Stretch	1	30 second hold
Kneeling Hip Flexor	1	30 second hold
Side Lunge Stretch	1	30 second hold
Lat Stretch w/ Physio– Ball	1	30 second hold
Chest Stretch w/ Physio-Ball	1	30 seconds hold

Functional Warm-up Exercises:	Sets:	Repetitions
Bent Knee Press Up	1	10
Flat Bench Hip Extension	1	10
Alternating Arm & Leg Extension	1	10
Thoracic Spine Openers	1	10
Plank Scapular Push Up	1	10
Forward Lunge w/ Reach	1	10
Inch Worm	1	10

Power Exercises:	Sets:	Repetitions:
Medicine Ball Side Throw	2	10
Squat Jumps	2	10
Medicine Bal Overhead Slam	2	10

Balance Exercises:	Sets:	Repetitions:
Balance Pad Single Leg Cone Reach	1	10
Balance Pad Single Leg Toe Touch	1	10

Core Strength Exercises:	Sets:	Repetitions:
Physio-Ball Circular Forearm Saws	2	15
Physio-Ball Leg Curl	2	15
Standing Cable Lifts	2	15
Standing Cable Chops	2	15

Scapular Integrity Exercises:	Sets:	Repetitions:
Physio-Ball Y-T-W-L	1	15

Functional Exercises:	Sets:	Repetitions:
Goblet Squat	3	8
Single Arm Physio-Ball DB Press	3	8
Single Leg DB Dead Lift	3	8
Pull Up	3	8

Anaerobic Conditioning:

60-yard Sprint Intervals (60 yard sprint, 20 seconds rest) x 6

Advanced Strength & Conditioning Program Two

Guidelines:

4 times per week	Alternate between Program A and B	1-3 sets per exercise	5-20 repetitions per set

Program A

Foam Roll Exercises:	Sets:	Repetitions:
Calf Foam Roll	1	5
Glute Foam Roll	1	5
IT Band Foam Roll	1	5
Adductors Foam Roll	1	5
Thoracic Foam Roll	1	5
Lat Foam Roll	1	5

Flexibility Exercises:	Sets:	Repetitions

90/90 Hamstring Stretch	1	30 second hold
Piriformis Stretch	1	30 second hold
Glute Stretch	1	30 second hold
Kneeling Hip Flexor	1	30 second hold
Side Lunge Stretch	1	30 second hold
Lat Stretch w/ Physio–Ball	1	30 second hold
Chest Stretch w/ Physio-Ball	1	30 seconds hold

Functional Warm-up Exercises:	**Sets:**	**Repetitions**
Bent Knee Press Up	1	10
Flat Bench Hip Extension	1	10
Alternating Arm & Leg Extension	1	10
Thoracic Spine Openers	1	10
Plank Scapular Push Up	1	10
Forward Lunge w/ Reach	1	10
Inch Worm	1	10

Power Exercises:	**Sets:**	**Repetitions:**
Medicine Ball Overhead Slam	3	10
Single Leg Box Jump	3	5

Balance Exercises:	**Sets:**	**Repetitions:**
Balance Pad Single Leg Airplane Rotations	1	10

Core Strength Exercises:	**Sets:**	**Repetitions:**
Physio-Ball Circular Forearm Saws	2	15
Physio-Ball Jack Knife	2	15
Physio-Ball Leg Curl	2	15

Functional Exercises:	**Sets:**	**Repetitions:**
Dumbbell Goblet Squat	3	8
Pull Up	3	8
Bulgarian Split Squat w/ DB	3	8
Single Arm DB Row	3	8

Anaerobic Conditioning:

60-yard Sprint Intervals (60 yard sprint, 20 seconds rest) x 6

Program B

Foam Roll Exercises:	Sets:	Repetitions:
Calf Foam Roll	1	5
Glute Foam Roll	1	5
IT Band Foam Roll	1	5
Adductors Foam Roll	1	5
Thoracic Foam Roll	1	5
Lat Foam Roll	1	5

Flexibility Exercises:	Sets:	Repetitions
90/90 Hamstring Stretch	1	30 second hold
Piriformis Stretch	1	30 second hold
Glute Stretch	1	30 second hold
Kneeling Hip Flexor	1	30 second hold
Side Lunge Stretch	1	30 second hold
Lat Stretch w/ Physio– Ball	1	30 second hold
Chest Stretch w/ Physio-Ball	1	30 seconds hold

Functional Warm-up Exercises:	Sets:	Repetitions
Bent Knee Press Up	1	10
Flat Bench Hip Extension	1	10
Alternating Arm & Leg Extension	1	10
Thoracic Spine Openers	1	10
Plank Scapular Push Up	1	10
Side Lung w/ Reach	1	10
Spider	1	10

Power Exercises:	Sets:	Repetitions:
Medicine Ball Side Throw	3	10
Medicine Ball Chest Throw	2	8

Balance Exercises:	Sets:	Repetitions:
Balance Pad Single Cone Reaches	1	10

| Balance Pad Single Leg Toe Touches | 1 | 10 |

Core Strength Exercises:	**Sets:**	**Repetitions:**
Standing Cable Chops	2	15
Standing Cable Lifts	2	15

Scapular Integrity Exercises:	**Sets:**	**Repetitions:**
Physio-Ball Y-T-W- L w/ 3 lb. DBs	1	10

Functional Exercises:	**Sets:**	**Repetitions:**
Barbell Dead Lift	3	8
Single Arm Physio-Ball DB Press	3	8
Single Leg DB Dead Lift	3	8
Kneeling Lunge OH DB Press	3	8

Summary

The final chapter of this book has provided you a comprehensive set of strength and conditioning programs. I suggest using these programs as samples for the development of your own individualized training program. Proceed at your own pace through the programs and use the time frames as guidelines only. A periodization schedule is integral in the development of a pitcher and should be followed.

Use all the information in this book to your benefit. Understand the importance of mobility, stability and power as it relates to baseball. Educate yourself on the training principles to adhere to as a golfer. Most of all enjoy the process of improving your golf game. Thank you for giving me the opportunity to assist you in this process.

About the Author

Sean Cochran is the Founder and Director of Sean Cochran Sports Peformance and one of the most recognized performance coaches in sport today. Sean began his career in professional athletics in 1999 as a strength and conditioning coach of the Milwaukee Brewers of Major League Baseball. Cochran transitioned from the Brewers to his adopted hometown of San Diego in 2000 where he accepted the position of Strength and Conditioning Coordinator for the San Diego Padres. During his tenure in Major League Baseball, Sean had the opportunity to train World Series MVP Cole Hamels, Cy Young Award Winners Barry Zito and Jake Peavy, and second in all time saves leader Trevor Hoffman.

Sean transitioned from professional baseball to professional golf in late 2003. Since this transition, Cochran has had the opportunity to work with numerous PGA Tour and LPGA players most notably 3-time Masters, PGA, and British Open Champion Phil Mickelson. In addition to Mickelson, Sean has worked with U.S. Open Champion Corey Pavin, PGA Tour and Senior U.S. Open Champion Peter Jacobsen, Ryder Cup Member and PGA Tour Winner Brad Faxon, PGA Championship Winner Shaun Michel, and LPGA Winners Hee Won Han, IK Kim, and Jennifer Johnson.

In addition to his work in professional athletics, Sean has authored and produced over 10 publications and numerous training videos related to sports performance training, has been a contributing author to PGATOUR.com, has served as a corporate ambassador to fortune 500 companies, product endorsee, and presenter at numerous educational seminars. Since the grand opening of Sean Cochran Sports Performance Training Facility, Sean has had the opportunity to train athletes in multiple sports including football, baseball, and golf with a focus on mentoring high school athletes.

Sean's accreditations include National Strength and Conditioning Association (1997), United States Weightlifting Federation (1998), American Sports Medicine Institute (1996), and the National Academy of Sports Medicine (2001, 2004).

COCHRAN'S STATS

- 8 Professional Golf Major Championships
- 2 CY Young Award Winners
- 7 MLB All Stars
- 4 Ryder Cup Team Members
- 5 President's Cup Team Members
- 8 first round MLB Draft Choices
- Multiple PGA Tour & LPGA Tour Winners
- Numerous MLB Draft Choices
- Multiple Division I Athletic Scholarship Recipients

Bibliography

Baechle, T.R., R.W. Earle, and D. Wathen. 2000 Resistance Training. In *Essentials of Strength Training and Conditioning* (2nd ed.), edited by T.R. Baechle and R.W. Earle. Champaign, IL: Human Kinetics

Boyle, M. 2004 Plyometric Training for Power, Targeted Torso Training and Rotational Strength. In *Functional Training for Sports*, edited by E. McNeely. Champaign, IL: Human Kinetics

Clark, M. 2001 Integrated Training, Human Movement Science, Current Concepts in Flexibility Training, Core Stabilization Training, Neuromuscular Stabilization Training. In *Integrated Training for the New Millennium*, edited by J. Jackson. Thousand Oaks, CA: National Academy of Sports Medicine

Cook, G. 2003 Mobility and Stability. In *Athletic Body in Balance*, edited by M. Barnard. Champaign, IL: Human Kinetics

Enoka, R. 1998 Human Movement Forces, Torque, Musckoskeletal Organization, Movement Strategies. In *Neuromechanical Basis of Kinesiology*, edited by R. Frey. Champaign, IL: Human Kinetics

Houglum, P. 2013 *An Analysis of the biomechanics of pitching in baseball,* Champaign, IL: Human Kinetics

House, T. 1994 Throwing the Ball: Deception, Energy Translation, Launch, and Deceleration. In *The Pitching Edge*, Champaign, IL: Human Kinetics

House, T. 1996 Rehabilitative Training. In *Fit to Hit,* Champaign, IL: Human Kinetics

Murphy, Forney. 1997 Benefits of Complete Conditioning for the Baseball Playe*r*. In *Complete Conditioning for Baseball*, Champaign, IL: Human Kinetics

Nicholls, R. L. 2006, "Numerical Analysis of maximal bat performance in baseball". *Journal of Biomechanics*

Reyes, Francis, October 2009, "Acute Effects of Various Weighted Bat Warm-Up Protocols on Bat Velocity". *Journal of Strength and Conditioning Research*

Santanna, J.C. 2004, Training Variables in *The Essence of Program Design*, Boca Rotan, FL: Optimum Performance Systems

Verstegen, M. Williams P., 2004 Movement Prep, Prehab, Elasticity in *Core Performance*, edited by J. Williams. United States of America: Rodale

Welch, C.M.; S.A. Banks, F.F. Dook, P. Draovitcg. 1995, "Hitting a Baseball: A Biomechanical Description". *Journal of Orthopaedic and Sport Physical Therapy*